THE PATH OF LIFE

Catherine Johnstone

The Path of Life

A biography of
Willie Johnstone's ministry
in Brazil and Scotland

by
Cathie Johnstone

LIFE-CHANGING BOOKS

First Published 1997 by Life-Changing Books
91 High Street, Weldon, NN17 3JJ, UK

British Library Cataloguing in Publication Data

A catalogue record of this book
is available from the British Library

ISBN   0 9530487 0 5

Typeset by Broad Bay Software Ltd
Production by Page '90 Publishing Consultants
Printed by Apollo Print & Design

Dedication

To the reader; may God help you to
find *The Path of Life* that leads to Eternal Life.

Foreword

There are some Christians whose God-given personality attracts others to the Christian faith. This outward appearance of inner contentment was possessed in no small degree by Willie Johnstone.

Although small in stature he was big in every other way. His voice was strong and melodious, a great asset in a preacher; this, combined with excellent content, relevant illustration and a controlled use of humour, resulted in a talented and much sought after preacher and speaker. No furtive glance at the watch when Willie Johnstone was preaching.

It was my privilege to be a friend of Willie during the later years of his life. I did not see him in action on the streets of Glasgow or the Amazon jungle but in the Kirk Session of St. Vincent Street Free Church in Glasgow. I was always impressed by his ability to choose his words carefully – he knew when to speak and he knew when to remain silent, a much more difficult exercise. He was not a contentious man and epitomised the adage *a soft word turneth away wrath.*

Cathie and Willie formed a true partnership in the Lord. They were an excellent double act for congregational fellowships and other such meetings, maintaining the interest of the audience by close interaction and appropriate illustration with the use of words and props. Their united aim was to attract others to their Saviour. It would have been a great loss if the life of Willie Johnstone had not been recorded for posterity. I am delighted that Cathie has accepted the challenge. She deserves our thanks and congratulations for lifting her pen when she was long beyond the threescore years and ten.

For Willie Johnstone, like the apostle Paul, to live was Christ and we have no doubt that for him, to die was gain. Although dead, his words and deeds live on. My hope and prayer is that through reading this book, others may come to know, love and follow that same Lord Jesus Christ who was always central in the long and varied life of Willie Johnstone.

Colin MacKay   FRCS
Elder, St Vincent Street Free Church, Glasgow

Acknowledgements

I am grateful and thankful for advice and help received from others at all stages of writing this book.

Mr Colin MacKay, my former elder at St. Vincent Street Free Church, Glasgow, encouraged me to put pen to paper; without which I would not have had the courage to begin the venture.

Friends and colleagues at the Unevangelized Fields Mission (UFM) have supported me throughout by searching filing cabinets and brains for details dimmed in my memory by the passage of time, and even sometimes completely forgotten!

My present minister, Rev Dr. D M MacDonald of Bishopbriggs Free Church, and many in my congregation have kept me going by their loving prayers and tokens of love when my strength and health have almost failed. I am strengthened by their belief that it is the Lord's will to have the tale told to his everlasting glory.

I thank my children and other relations for putting up with my obsessive behaviour. They have endured my long months of labour with pen and paper, and graciously agreed to have certain aspects of their personal lives revealed in this book.

I extend special thanks to Pam Wood, Alex Stewart and David Page; they undertook the time-consuming task of typing and editing the text and typesetting it in preparation for the publishers.

My prayer is that God will bless this book to some precious soul and to those in need of guidance as to which *Path of Life* to follow.

Cathie Johnstone, 1997.

Bibliography

Treks at Home & Abroad, 1931, Missionary Training Colony Publication, Battley Brothers, The Queensgate Press, Clapham Park.

South America – A Complete Guide, Fodor 93.

Glasgow Evening Citizen.

Amazon Beaming, Petru Popescu, MacDonald, 1991.

The Fate of the Forest, Developers, Destroyers and Defenders, Susan Hecht & Alexander Cockburn, Verso, 1989.

The Amazon Rain Forest and its People, Marion Morrison, Wayland, 1993.

Introduction

Willie Johnstone, my husband, died in 1990 at the age of eighty. His life was dedicated to the Lord, both at home in Scotland and in missionary service in Brazil. Many who knew Willie wished that he would put pen to paper and record his experiences.

Since his passing, I have had numerous requests to carry out this work, and it is with prayerful consideration that I now do so.

I trust that God will bless that which He enabled Willie and me to do in His Name, and that this book will be a blessing to many in years to come.

1. Early Days

Speechless Willie

"Young man, are you going to Heaven?" The young eighteen-year-old lad thought to himself that since he was speaking to the new minister he had better say "Yes", which he did. Following hard on that response the minister then asked, "And on what authority are you going there?" The boy was speechless—for he had *no* authority to say so.

That speechless lad was William "Willie" Johnstone, born on 19 February 1910, in the Springburn district of Glasgow; one of a family of nine children. His hard-working parents were members of the Church of Scotland in Blochairn, Garngad, Glasgow.

When a new minister, the Reverend Arthur Wallace, was inducted into Blochairn, he began visitation of all lapsed members, being a godly and conscientious pastor. On calling at the Johnstone home he found that the parents were out; only Willie, with his brother David and two of David's friends, were present to welcome the new minister.

When David realised the situation he and his friends excused themselves, leaving Willie alone with the minister. Reverend Wallace was a faithful servant of God, true to his calling as a minister of the Gospel – he did not discuss trivial matters but asked Willie that very piercing question: "Young man, are you going to Heaven?"

The minister read from the Bible and left some helpful booklets. Before leaving the house he knelt down and prayed. This impressed Willie very much and after the minister left Willie too was on his knees confessing his sin before Almighty God and asking God to come into his life.

A great transformation took place; his prayer was answered and he knew he was a 'new creation.'

The Best News of All!

It is good to pass on good news – and here was the best news of all! Willie told David, and as time progressed his brother saw a change in Willie's behaviour and lifestyle. David too was converted and with their new outlook they felt constrained to pray for their parents.

The home circumstances were difficult. For example, in extremely cold weather there was little heating in the home – but the brothers would huddle under blankets for warmth, and there they would pray. Over the years, God mercifully answered their prayers; both their parents were converted, as were a number of their brothers and sisters.

Within one year of Willie and David's conversion, their mother met a neighbour whilst out shopping who invited her to the women's meeting at the Railway Mission, Vulcan Street, Springburn. She was converted on that very day after hearing the message given by a dear saint of God. Eight year's later Willie's father was converted at the same Railway Mission. Special services were being held for a month; many from the neighbourhood came also and were converted.

Rev. A E Wallace MA

Archie, the youngest son in the family, was converted as a young lad through the instrumentality of those importunate prayers of Willie and David. I remember Archie turning over the pages of his Bible and saying to Willie, "Where in the Bible does it say: 'Go ye into all the world and preach the gospel to every creature'?" It was especially encouraging to note his interest in God's Word at such an early age – no-one could possibly know at this time, but in God's plan Archie was to be taken into Glory in the very prime of life.

The children were all trained at an early age to be independent. Although Willie had sisters he even did his own laundry, and there was no drip-dry clothing in those days! He disliked school, even though he had the ability for study. He would absent himself from school without his parents' knowledge, until the School Board man appeared on the doorstep, giving his mother quite a shock. University or further study was not at all in his thoughts and he left school when about sixteen years of age, attaining to a Day School Higher Certificate.

Zeal for the Lord

George Stewart, a school friend, invited Willie and David to the Railway Mission in Vulcan Street, Springburn. They started to attend all the worship services, and were watched over by a very godly Superintendent, Mr George Scott. This Hall had an appointed Secretary who would arrange for various preachers to conduct the services week by week. There would be a congregation of about seventy attending regularly, mostly young people and some with young families – all very zealous for the Lord.

Mr Scott served his apprenticeship in the shipyard on the Clyde and so used his skills in a God-glorifying way to train those teenage boys. He held woodwork classes in the mission for young men wanting to learn the skills. The finished articles were sold in aid of the church buildings and missions abroad. At the same time, he made sure they understood the Gospel.

Sewing Bees were very popular at this time in Glasgow. Ladies of all ages would meet together weekly in their local mission hall or church and spend the evening knitting or sewing; some places even had sewing machines available to use. Hidden talents were found as a variety of dresses, blouses, skirts, shirts, trousers, jumpers and cardigans were gladly made and sent to various mission fields abroad.

The Christian Endeavour was a great help to the young people. Meetings consisted of passing on a word on the topic for that evening, taken from the Word of God. There was organised chain praying and two working committees, namely, the Missionary Committee and the Lookout (Witness) Committee. It truly was a good place for young people to pray publicly, perhaps for the first time; there was real commitment to the work. Even the weekly notices were given out with the exhortation "do plan to be with us."

The Missionary Vision

Every Sunday morning at ten o'clock there was a missionary prayer meeting. Missionary letters were read with a different country being prayed for each week. The Superintendent had a great missionary vision; before taking charge of this mission he had trained to be a missionary for Africa. Sadly, his health did not allow him to go to the field; nevertheless, he still had the vision of a perishing world and many were influenced by his leadership and prayers.

Even in those early days Willie loved to preach in the open air and in the back courts of tenement buildings. Prayer and witnessing were foremost in Willie's daily life. He truly had a concern for the people who had no thought for God. **Before** Saturday and Sunday evening services there was a season of prayer; this was the best preparation one could have had for God's work.

Lots of people walked up and down Springburn Road aimlessly. On one occasion, from the crowds, two ladies stopped to listen and were truly apprehended by the Spirit of God. They realised how they could be assured of their sins to be forgiven, if they but confessed their utter dependence on the shed blood of Jesus Christ on Calvary's cross. They became ardent members of the Mission.

Whenever there was a missionary prayer meeting Willie would be there; particularly at missionary rallies where perhaps a missionary home on furlough would tell what God had done through their witness.

Willie felt the need to study the Bible and so he went to Glasgow Bible Training Institute evening classes for four years. His desire for missionary work was unabated.

2. Call to the Mission Field & Preparation

The Plight of the Indians

Willie's first job was in an office for about one year as an office boy. When he was thinking of leaving this job, Willie had to do much heart-searching. Now that he was a Christian, he realised he should have a clear conscience before God and men. His conscience was truly pricked because he had pilfered some stamps; but restitution was made to his employer.

Shortly afterwards he answered an advertisement for a fish salesman in the Glasgow Fish Market and was successful in getting the post. By the standards of that time he had a very good job, with excellent pay, plus commission, and he enjoyed his work there very much. His family appreciated his financial contribution during the depression of the 1930s, as he alone was working.

In his new job at the fishmarket, he could have afforded public transport but he walked to work every day from Balornock in the Springburn district of Glasgow to the market on the south side of the city. The sole reason for this was to save money for missionary support.

Then came a great challenge. In a meeting at the Anniesland Hall, Glasgow, Mrs C. T. Studd of the World Evangelisation Crusade (WEC) spoke about the plight of the Indians on the Amazon River in Brazil. This was a very special meeting – the Spirit of God made it plain to Willie that he was being called to serve in Brazil!

His mother was devastated at the prospect of losing his income; Willie's decision exercised the faith of the whole family. However, the call to the mission field was loud and clear.

He went on to make enquiries about entering the Missionary service. He had heard good reports about the

Missionary Training Colony in Highfield Hill, Upper Norwood, London. He was so confident of his call that he made application to be trained for pioneer missionary service amongst the redskin Indians of Brazil.

His application was successful, and he resigned from his job. When Willie was initially interviewed, his boss had instructed him that "the biggest lie was the best lie." Willie, as a Christian, did not value this philosophy, and his witness was such that his boss presented him with a very special study Bible when he left.

Spiritual Commandos

Willie left home with £15 in his pocket which was the fee charged for entry to the Missionary Training College. He left behind all home comforts of Scotland for the pioneer camp in England where he would be staying.

The vision for the camp came from two men who were dear saints of God, namely Captain B. Godfrey Buxton and Mr A. V. Blackwell. The whole set-up was spiritual, disciplined and most practical.

The Colony treks were primarily for training purposes, and for the development of the members of the party. They required perseverance for the daily routine of striking camp and marching to the next location; they had to contend with the weather, fatigue, hilly terrain and also temptation – the kindness of friends would tempt them to linger. However, new friends awaited, and the Gospel had to be preached at a new location: the work had to continue.

The trekkers learned to work together, to be adaptable, patient, using only that which was needed to promote the good of the party and for the sake of the work. There was a continual turning to the Lord for direction, inspiration, and strength; He never failed.

One of the men who shared this experience with Willie was Fred Wright, who also went to serve the Lord in Brazil.

The Pioneer Camp

The day started at 6am in the Pioneer Camp. Five minutes after rising, the trainees took part in tough muscle-building exercises followed quickly by a plunge into near-freezing water.

The camp itself had no luxuries; in fact the trainees had to build huts, pipe water and lay drains. A spell in the Casualty Department of Croydon Hospital provided them with essential first aid and basic surgery skills; they knew how to pull teeth with make-shift forceps, and how to set a broken bone.

Self-sufficiency was the goal; with only a tent, a hand cart and basic cooking equipment, the trainees, now trekkers, would set off in pairs into the countryside. They would learn to exist on a minimum of food.

Trekkers with bikes went ahead

An important part of the training – and a clue to their ultimate battleground – was fashioning a dugout canoe and learning all they could about tropical diseases. A visitor to the pioneer camp would notice a significant difference between these commandos and some of the hard-bitten wartime variety. Nobody was ever heard to use a swear word and they didn't smoke or drink.

During vacation in the summer months various treks were organised in England, Wales, Scotland and Ireland. These personal contacts with so many people of all age groups offered a wonderful opportunity for open-air witness. "You will be different men when you get back!" was the rather alarming remark made by an older trekker to some new ones before they set out.

Later they would be praising God for the truth of that statement; they were different men – toughened in physique, strengthened in character, enlarged in experience and above all imperishably enriched in the experiential knowledge of the Living God.

God's Cheques

The Welsh Trek presented an interesting problem to the prospective pioneer. The route started in Swindon and ran through Gloucester, right round the south coast of Wales, through Cardiff, Swansea and Milford Haven and up to Aberystwyth where they turned inland to Shrewsbury and Birmingham and then back to Swindon; a total distance of 560 miles. The country west of Cardiff had not been covered before by the Colony and it was quite unknown to all of them. Moreover, it was peopled by folk of a very different temperament and in many places they spoke a different language. Looking back now one sees how wonderfully God undertook as they lived a day at a time and trusted Him for that day. In the second half of the trek the purse usually contained far more of 'God's cheques' than actual money, but they always had enough and in the end (like the disciples of old) they brought back more than they started with. God's cheques were not always hard cash but other expressions of God's bounty.

God was thanked for every remembrance of the Lord's people who in many places opened their hearts and homes to them and with whom they had happy fellowship. It rained, and there were hills – but that served to build up their resilience and character.

In one place some of the team slept in a cowshed – without the cows it is only fair to add! They thanked God for the privilege of seeing the fruit of their labour; people had their lives changed, becoming new creations in Christ. The bulk of the ministry was in the open-air; there and indoors the Lord was pleased to bless them to an unusual degree – souls being touched by personal witness in the power of the Holy Spirit.

About twenty thousand Gospels, tracts and scripture portions were distributed. *Precious seed* for which they were deeply indebted to the Scripture Gift Mission. As they united in praising God for all his blessing, they prayed not to forget to pray that He would establish and make fruitful all that was done in His Name.

The Scottish Trek

Willie always remembered with thankfulness an outstanding home that was opened to them in a little village on the Scottish Trek. It belonged to Mr and Mrs David MacKie, owners of the grocer's shop and adjoining house at the corner of Buchanan Street, Balfron, Stirlingshire.

The students journeyed in pairs. One night, Willie and his companion had to sleep in a barn. They were not keen to spend another night in such conditions, so, on the next day, Willie travelled ahead by bicycle in search of accommodation. His companion, pulling the hand cart with all their meagre belongings, would arrive later.

When Willie arrived in Balfron he saw some children playing in the street. He asked them, "Do you know of any Christians in this village?" The children unhesitatingly responded "Oh yes, Mr and Mrs MacKie at the shop in this very street." Willie knocked on the door and before he could complete a sentence Mrs MacKie said "Are you from the London Training Colony? I've heard all about you boys.   Come away in and this will be your home for as long as you need!" This was to be only one of many homes that were at the disposal of the boys.

They also experienced testing times, and all these events continued to strengthen their characters, enabling them to face all kinds of situations in the future on the mission field.

One highlight of the Scottish Trek was in the town of Ayr. They met a fine-art dealer who was a committed Christian; on learning about their recent camp experiences, he promptly arranged for them to have high tea in a local restaurant. After tea, the proprietor informed them that arrangements had been made for them to have their meals there for the next week! The boys were stunned by this generosity.

Willie (centre) with hand cart behind

During Willie's first furlough from Brazil he received an invitation to speak at the Ayrshire Christian Union. He accepted the invitation and as a result interest in the work of Unevangelised Fields Mission Worldwide (UFM) grew, and friendships deepened; that same generous gentleman arranged to pay for all of Willie's film on his return to Brazil.

Years later, when Willie was Deputation Secretary, our family was invited to the Ayrshireman's home. We met his wife and daughter and enjoyed a lovely meal and warm fellowship. After the meal, I was taken upstairs and shown many lovely garments. We were given clothes for me and the family, and also a beautiful down quilt with matching bedspread.   They produced an empty pigskin suitcase and proceeded to fill it with clothes. Look at what is said in Luke 6:38:

> *Give, and it shall be given unto you; good measure, pressed down, and shaken together, and running over, shall men give into your bosom. For with the same measure that you use withal it shall be measured to you again.*

It was around midnight when we arrived home that night; we were so thrilled with the gifts that we had received that we could not wait to try them and, despite the lateness of the hour, we had our own little fashion parade.

This support continued over many years, both in the field and at home.

Training Complete

On completion of this three-year training, Willie applied to UFM for work amongst the savage Indians on the Amazon River in Brazil.   During his interview with the Council in London he was asked how he would contend with the difficulties if full allowances were not forthcoming! His faith was strong and he truly believed that his God would supply all his need. Those very early days of mission were truly hard, but within Willie's soul there was such a peace and joy in knowing that God had counted him worthy to serve Him.

3. Brazil at last!

The Brazil of 1994

Recife is the capital of the state of Pernambuco and the true capital of the Brazilian Northeast. The sixth largest city in Brazil, with a population of 1.5 million, Recife is a vibrant metropolis whose spirit is halfway between the modern cities of the south and the more traditional centres of the Northeast. Known as the Venice of Brazil because it is built on three rivers and connected by a host of bridges, Recife got its name from the reefs that line the coast and make the city's most popular beach, Boa Viagam, also one of the more unusual bathing spots in Brazil.

Fortaleza – capital of the state of Ceara, this city of 1.8 million, fifth largest in Brazil. The city has excellent attractions – fine beaches and even better ones located nearby, the best lobster fishing and eating in Brazil and the top lace industry in the country. The city is also on its way to becoming a world-class fashion centre, thanks to the combination of abundant raw materials and cheap manpower.

Belem – the city of Belem is the gateway to the Amazon, 90 miles from the open sea. Ultra-modern high-rises dot the horizon, mingling with older red-tiled buildings. Belem was the first centre of European colonisation in the Amazon. The Portuguese settled here in 1616 using the city as a jumping off point for the interior jungle region and also as an outpost to protect the mouth of the Amazon River. Although Belem today is a bustling, modern city, the influence of the Amazon river and jungle remains strong. Despite its international airport, the city still depends heavily on the river for contact with the outside world. The highway to Brasilia was built to end Belem's isolation from the rest of the country but it is still a seasonal highway subject to periodic closures because of heavy rains and flooding along the route.

Manaus – a sprawling city of nearly one million, built in the densest part of the jungle, Manaus has re-established its role as the key city of the Amazon basin after years of dormancy (the long hoped-for expansion of the Amazon basin did not attain the desired results despite the inauguration of seasonal road connections with Belem and Brasilia).

The Brazil of 1934

Willie's eventual destination was a world apart from the modern day image of Brazil. Not for Willie the vibrant and sophisticated cities, landscaped by beautiful tree-lined beaches and high rise buildings. Willie was headed for the starkly different beauty of the Amazon Jungle with its dense rain forests and primitive isolation from the outside world.

He sailed for Brazil in one of the Booth Line steamers and spent a year at the mission base at Belem in the state of Para studying the Portuguese language. Willie left Liverpool accompanied by Mr and Mrs Harry Heath, who

were experienced missionaries in Brazil and were returning there following furlough.

Words failed to express the inner joy that Willie had
now that the time had come for the fulfilment of his one
ambition to serve Christ in Brazil. He now had to adapt to
a different climate – mosquitoes and primitive living
conditions – mosquitoes and new foods – mosquitoes and
a strange language. Once outside the mission base, the
Portuguese language was the only means of communica-
tion.

Mosquitoes were probably the greatest difficulty. They
were there for 24 hours a day, all the year round, and he
quickly appreciated the protection of the net at night. The
weather did not present too much of a problem, although
it was certainly hotter, more humid and the rain much
heavier than in Scotland! He also had to get used to
wearing a helmet on his head – not to keep warm or dry
as here at home, but to keep the sun's rays from burning
the skin and causing sunstroke.

Willie enjoyed much of the food, especially the wide
variety of fruits which he had never tasted before. Mangoes were his favourite: they were delicious. One missionary remarked to Willie that they were so juicy it would be
better to eat them in the bathroom! Pork was a problem to
him and he avoided eating it if possible. Pigs roamed
unattended everywhere and when he saw them feeding
amongst all sorts of waste he could not face a meal of this
type of animal.

As at any training centre, the base had its routine for
the day. Breakfast was at 7am. Before every meal of the
day grace was said in Portuguese. Those newly arrived
from Britain were allowed to read the words but soon they
were able to say it without help. After breakfast, Mr Harris
or one of the missionaries gave an exposition from Scripture for 10 to 15 minutes and for half-an-hour they engaged in prayer. The students then helped to tidy their

rooms and this was followed by a language lesson by Mr and Mrs Harris.

Dinner was at 11.30am. This meal consisted of sweet potato or rice with a variety of vegetables and meat. There were no fancy puddings but the fruit bowl was always full of fresh fruit which was a very healthy part of the diet. Dinner was followed by a rest (siesta) for an hour. At first it seemed strange to be lying down in the middle of the day but it soon became obvious how helpful this was when the midday sun was beating down. Brazilians would call it madness to walk about or shop at such a hot time of the day. After the rest there was a welcome cup of tea, coffee or *assaie*, which is a deep purple drink from the fruit of the same name derived from the palm tree. The fruit is squeezed and put through a sieve. Ice cream is also made from this very nutritious fruit.

Further language study would follow for the new recruits. This meant spending most of the afternoon going over the morning lesson – and previous ones, too! After a few months the new recruits would visit Christians in the surrounding area, practising their new language skills. Later still, unmarried missionaries were boarded out into Brazilian Christian homes, so that they would not speak English.

Evening meals were at 6pm as the sun went down. On the menu would be items such as fish, eggs rice, macaroni – yes, of course such menus existed over 50 years ago!

Following the evening meal, they would go for a short walk for about half an hour. On meetings nights the walk was far from short – the little church was located in the suburbs. In the outskirts there were no pavements; they walked on sand which slowed progress and seemed to add miles to the journey.

On arrival at the meetings they were overjoyed to see the church packed with people who were hungering and thirsting for God's Word; this was more than compensation for the long walks. Then there were also letters to type and sermons to prepare. Bedtime was usually 9.30 or 10pm.

While in training, Willie bought a pair of white buckskin shoes for Sunday services thinking they would combine well with the white starched suits that were worn to church by pastors and most missionaries. He wore these shoes to his first Portuguese church service. At the end of the day Willie carefully put his buckskin shoes on a shelf to be ready for the next Sunday services. Next Sunday, when he lifted down the shoes, he discovered that ants had been working overtime and nothing was left of his beautiful shoes but a twisted shell betraying none of their former glory.

Evangelisation

To be a messenger of the Gospel of Jesus Christ to the Indians is a privilege indeed. The missionaries encountered a people who lived in spiritual darkness, constantly in fear of evil spirits.

The Word of God was preached daily and the sacrificial death of Jesus was depicted using visual aids. There was an emphasis on creation; the Indians were taught that God had created a world of breath-taking diversity and wonders, into which He then placed Adam and Eve. The Indians can immediately identify with this God who has made their world, and has made them.

Through this preaching and witness, the Indians became aware of the demands God makes upon all of us. The work of the cross of Jesus Christ was constantly laid before them and, by the Spirit's work, they give their lives to God.

Pacification of the Indians

Before meeting the natives face-to-face, weeks were spent, maybe even months, leaving little gifts of food and trinkets on branches of trees beside jungle tracks. When it was thought they knew they were meant no harm, an attempt was made at a first tentative contact, indicating friendliness from a distance in the universal manner by showing they carried no weapons. Pacification can take a very long time and it could take many months before the chief was finally met.

The leaving of gifts is not an inherited tradition – the Indians themselves insist on it. The tradition, called *trocar presentes*, can be traced back to Columbus' first voyage, but the Indians have always exchanged gifts among themselves; they insisted on receiving gifts from newcomers, even if they did not really want them.

Domestication

Domestication of the Indians may sound easy – just a case of improving the standard of living of the tribe and providing medicine for the sick. However, at times it could be harrowing. The Kayapo, especially, were slow to change. For a time, during the period of domestication, the killing went on. It was not unusual for a child to be dashed against a tree to stop it crying during the night.

The missionary introduced hygiene, improved moral and living standards; there was no intention to change their culture. In fact, the Indians were able to teach the missionaries many things: jungle life, fishing methods, hunting methods and how to grow crops in the thin jungle soil.

The Indians have an extensive knowledge of herbal medicine; these remedies have the desired effect of treating particular illnesses.

However, very often Indians were attracted to spiritism involving dramatic scenes of tapping the body at the part which was painful, and blowing smoke from pipes placed at their mouths – puffing vigorously.

Indian witchdoctors, or *shamans,* would locate fractures by gently pulling on limbs; they would clean wounds by sucking out maggots and other foreign bodies – these foreign bodies they called demons. To the Indians, all objects are inhabited by spirits, with household objects having the strongest and most jealous.

The Guajajaras

Towards the end of 1935 Willie started working with a tribe of Indians called the Guajajaras in the neighbouring state of Maranhao – well away from the nearest point of civilisation. It was this remote work that had made the training in self-sufficiency so necessary. The Guajajara Indians were primitive, though not so hostile as some, but the work of pacification was difficult and sometimes dangerous. Missionaries had to build their own quarters and live off the land, shooting birds and animals for the pot.

Massacre

About this time three other missionaries, Fred Roberts from Australia, Fred Dawson from Tasmania and Fred Wright from Belfast, Northern Ireland – the Three Freds – all had a vision and a call from God to take the Gospel to the Kayapo Indians.

A year had passed since they had set out on this very dangerous expedition and fears were rising in London and at the mission base in Belem for their safety. An urgent message was sent to Horace Banner, Senior Missionary, and Willie, from the Mission in London and the base at Belem, to return to base at once.

Wright   Roberts   Dawson

Once there, they were asked to lead a search party of nine Brazilians to that point of the Xingu River called the *Cachoeira Grande*, meaning Big Rapid, having been advised to continue with caution and not to take unnecessary risks.

Before setting out on the search Mr Harris, the Field Leader, committed them to God in prayer and gave them a text for every day, to cover the whole of that very dangerous journey.

The following is an extract from a personal interview between Willie and a *Glasgow Evening Citizen* reporter, which appeared on 7th January, 1974:

> Any encyclopaedia will tell you about the conditions in the Amazonian rain forest, its high humidity, monotonously high temperatures, the tangled confusion of the oldest and densest vegetation in the world. Here you have one-third of the entire world's forestry and the Amazon itself "Rei Dos Rios" (King of the Rivers) contains one fifth of the world's fresh water. At the estuary the river is 210 miles wide and one of its main tributaries, the Xingu, winds south, through a series of spectacular rapids into the Mato Grosso, for 1,300 miles. Everything in this part

of Brazil – the Green Hell of Hollywood movies – is bigger and more profuse than in any other part of the globe. Botanists would revel in the fantastic variety of plant life. Within a few square miles could be found 700 different species of butterfly. Nobody who ventured there was terribly taken with the other fauna. Little fish: the voracious piranha with the scissor-like teeth which are capable of stripping the flesh from an alligator in seconds. Big snakes: among the constrictors is the 30 feet anaconda, able to swallow a horse! Rodents: the heavyweight champion rat, the capybara, four feet long and weighing seven stones.

The search for the Three Freds got under way at the tail end of the Monsoon, January 1936. Willie Johnstone and Horace Banner travelled first by river steamer from Belem, round the island of Marajo (incidentally the size of Switzerland) and up the Amazon. They left the Amazon and joined the Xingu River at Porto da Mos, and travelled by launch to Victoria. Here they left the river temporarily and travelled overland by lorry to Altamira to avoid the rapids. Back on the Xingu they carried on by launch up the longest stretch of the river to Bocadorio, nearing the most central part of Brazil, the heart of the rain forest. When they arrived at Bocadorio, which means mouth of the river, it was nothing more than a street of palm thatch huts. Its importance was that it had a police point, the last in fact in the state of Para. Beyond this point there was only the law of the jungle. It was there they recruited the Brazilian search party, river dwellers and more Negro than Portuguese, who scratched a living from rubber, Brazil nuts and hunting game. They had been persuaded in advance to co-operate in this expedition by a friend of the Fields Mission, a Para police chief, who sent word to Bocadorio. I suppose in the circumstances the river men felt it politic to help them out. They needed their knowledge of the Xingu river and jungle lore for they had to exist on fish, deer and birds. There is not much room in a canoe for packed provisions! The nine Brazilians were friendly enough but they made no pretence of their reluctance to penetrate beyond Cachoeira Grande, the big falls. At that time all of this territory was unexplored.

When the Kayapo tribe was mentioned the Brazilians demanded guns and the missionaries had to agree and gave each one a Winchester 44 with a box of bullets. Horace and Willie had only a revolver between them – protection against the jaguar and puma – which they did not expect to use, and certainly not on any human. The armed guides were brave men but by nature highly strung and liable to shoot in panic. They had had occasional encounters with hostile tribes and according to Francisco, the most talkative of the Brazilians, the Kayapo were a nasty lot schooled to kill. It was true that killing was written into their culture. Indeed, until he had taken a human life the Kayapo Indian was not allowed to sport the tattooed V on the chest, signifying warrior. However, as Christians the missionaries could not venture in on a lesser basis than the motto of the Indian Protection Society, "Die if necessary, kill never". As a result they were regarded by the river dwellers as a bit naive, if not unbalanced.

The two missionaries and the guides piled into three canoes, in each a Brazilian steersman and two paddlers; the missionaries adding extra paddle power when the current got tough. They carried hammocks, mosquito nets and what medical aids were available in the Thirties, mainly quinine to combat malarial fever. It was to be a two-stage journey. Stage one was Fresco, a little tributary as yet unmapped of the Xingu, about 1,000 miles into the bush. They paddled for four days, at night slinging their hammocks between trees on the river bank, trying to catch sleep amid a great cacophony of jungle cries. They dined on farinha, a kind of meal made from the tapioca plant; fish, birds and occasionally slices of roast *peccary* – wild pig. At the end of Stage one, the big rapids at Riozinho, they ran into trouble. They landed and prepared to hump the canoes round the falls. Suddenly the guides became very agitated. They had spotted a number of little palm-thatch huts and started back for the river. When asked what was the trouble the answer given was "Kayapo! Kayapo!" They said the huts belonged to the savages who could not be far away and who they were sure were watching them from the undergrowth. Fearing ambush they decided to clear out. When they took to the canoes, the hearts of the missionaries plummeted. They knew they would have to go all the way back and recruit another search party.

This extract appeared on 8 January 1974:

All in all they lost a week during the turn-round, but eventually they arrived back at Cachoeira Grande this time with a different plan. With the new search party they had a launch as well as canoes. When they disembarked at the falls to do the overland trek they decided to leave two men with the launch in case they were ambushed and had to make a sudden return without the canoes to the river. As it turned out they encountered no opposition and arrived at Stage two, Cachoeira Da Fumaca, The Smoke Falls, so called because of the great cloud of spray rising hundreds of feet above the jungle. It was the dry season and the river had fallen considerably. It was this that made it possible for them to make their first tragic discovery. At this spot, 1,000 miles from mission headquarters at Belem, they saw the boat that had been used by the missing missionaries. The prow was just visible above the water. A closer inspection revealed that it had been smashed and sunk.

This discovery created an eerie atmosphere. There was a strong feeling among the guides that the people responsible (the Kayapo tribesmen) were still present, watching from the bush, and a considerable amount of persuasion was necessary to hold on to the search party. The missionaries needed more evidence, though the possibility of finding the Three Freds alive seemed remote.

The Brazilians stayed by the canoes while the intrepid pair pushed into the bush. They had only gone a few hundred yards when they found the first clues – blood stained clothing, partly shredded by white ants. They made a similar discovery on the opposite bank of the river and were able to piece together what had happened when the Kayapo set eyes on the first white men. In that fateful encounter, nearly a year previously (at the end of 1934) two of the missionaries, probably Fred Roberts and Fred

Dawson, had left the canoe and gone forward to the spot where they found the first lot of tattered clothing. The Kayapo Indians, schooled to kill would not have hesitated. The two men had been clubbed to death. The second find of clothing on the opposite bank indicated that the third missionary had been overwhelmed trying to make his escape in the canoe.

Why?

Their first fears now realised they stood in a sacred silence reflecting much on their brothers in Christ who had not counted their lives dear to themselves. There seems always to be the question, Why? Why? Why? How can we face questions about this waste of precious life? What keeps the child of God from despair in the midst of suffering?

This harrowing experience produced an indelible mark on the lives of Horace and Willie and for the relatives and friends who deeply mourned the loss.

Willie himself knew the answer and he preached to this effect from 2 Corinthians 4:16–18:

> *For which cause we faint not; but though our outward man perish, yet the inward man is renewed day by day.*
>
> *For our light affliction, which is but for a moment, worketh for us a far more exceeding and eternal weight of glory;*
>
> *While we look not at the things which are seen, but at the things which are not seen: for the things which are seen are temporal; but the things which are not seen are eternal.*

The apostle Paul counted affliction to be light while we poor souls may think it burdensome. Affliction is for a moment, working for us a far more exceeding and eternal weight of Glory. The natural man says "How could that possibly be?" See how affliction works, giving a far more exceeding and eternal weight of glory while we look not at the things which are seen but at the things which are not seen. The things which we see are temporal but the things which are not seen are everlasting. What is your perspective of the future? Derive comfort and hope from the above verses.

Horace, Willie and the guides now began their journey back downstream gripped with shock, fear and tension. Their restful spirit was gone as they suffered lack of sleep and hunger.

What makes the missionary life bearable? It is not an adventure as many think but a constraint by the Holy Spirit to preach the Gospel to every creature, nothing daunting.

Can you visualise the crew arriving at Belem at the end of that harrowing experience? I am sure they sighed with relief to be safely returned to base with hearts full of praise to God for His guiding and protective hand in the most dangerous situation. The prayers of God's people had been continually besieging the Throne and a gracious answer had been given.

How we thanked God for the safety of the search party. Soon news of the martyrdom of Roberts, Wright and Dawson was getting a hearing in churches throughout Britain and this proved a tremendous impetus for the mission.

You might say it put UFM on the evangelical map. They received support, financial and otherwise, to push on with the work in Brazil and recruitment increased markedly.

4. The Multi-role Missionary

The Urubu Indians

Following this harrowing experience Horace, Willie and the crew needed rest and building up because of weight lost due to energy expended on the trip.

After the day's activities were over, these single young men would go down to the river to bathe. Willie told me that on one occasion he gave one of the Indians some of his clothing to be washed. Very soon he noticed the young Indian dressed up in one of his shirts; he soaped it all up – then dived into the river. That is one way to wash away your worries about washing your clothes!

When Willie had recovered, he undertook a journey into the Maranhao jungle, accompanied by an Irish missionary, Frank Houston. This took two weeks by train and launch, including one called *Boas Novas*, which means Good News. Then, Willie made his second contact – the Urubu tribe.

The Tembe language and a little Portuguese were spoken here. The conditions were truly primitive; houses had the usual thatched roofs and mud floors, the dining room had walls to a height of only four feet. Privacy was minimal for them as there were few doors in their accommodation. However, the missionaries' house was situated in the jungle and there were lovely fruit trees everywhere, yielding an abundance of mangoes, bananas, oranges and lemons, to name but a few.

Later, they were joined by Leslie Goodman. The three missionaries were all single men then; they laboured with dedication to bring the Gospel to those who were sitting in darkness and superstition. The openness of their house unfortunately led to Leslie Goodman being bitten on the ear by a bat one night while sleeping. This caused a fair loss of blood and his health deteriorated. His furlough was nearly due, so the mission returned him to base early. Frank and Willie continued the work.

There were sixty Urubus in the village; men, women and children. They would gather every morning at the home of the missionaries for worship. Some had already been awakened to their need of a Saviour. It was wonderful indeed to see God's Spirit working in the dark places of the earth.

These Indians had to be fed and clothed, hence it was desirable to employ them usefully in certain tasks. Some would go into the plantation to attend to the crops of rice, beans and so on. Others would take to the river and fish and those who could hunt would venture farther into the jungle for meat.

The Maranatha

The men on the compound helped the missionaries to make a launch. There were no trading posts or shops so they were dependent on the men returning with supplies;

the launch would be packed with canned food, flour, salt and cloth to make clothes, and other goodies previously unknown in the area.

The sun rose at 6am and went down at 6pm every day. During November the rainy season would arrive; it would last until January – tropical rain is something to behold, so ferocious no raincoat could keep one dry!

Joyful and Sorrowful News

Mail was always eagerly awaited. It was such a joy and a great uplift to the missionaries' spirits to receive many kind words from their relatives and friends, encouraging them to press on even when the going was hard.

At home, letters from the field made sad reading: war, murder, persecution and suffering abounded. Joys and sorrows were abundantly mixed in the life of the pioneer missionary, or anyone who was engaged in Gospel witness.

One of these sorrows was that Willie's house was burned to the ground with the total loss of all his equipment because of a weasel chasing some chickens. One of the Indians foolishly gave chase with a firebrand that accidentally set fire to the dry straw roof.

There stood Willie, the only clothing left to him was what he was wearing – and he would now have to grow his beard!

His greatest loss was his well-marked study Bible: one of the Council members from London was on a visit to the field at that particular time and he kindly gifted Willie with a Bible identical to the one lost. Everything is mixed with the mercy of our God who knows us as individuals and supplies our needs.

In those early days there were few teaching aids. Flannelgraph, filmstrips and a blackboard were, however, all available for use. In the evening, with a Tilly lamp providing excellent light, the missionaries would sit to teach many of these Indians the Bible.

Tommy Who?

It was the habit of these Indians to journey through the jungle to visit other villages; this would take several days. There were twenty outlying villages and the missionaries planned to visit these whenever possible. On one particular journey of this sort Willie accompanied the men; this was a wonderful opportunity for witness.

Tomehu & Willie

In one village they met Tomehu, pronounced *Tommy Who*, a big naked warrior with the tail feather of a macaw pushed through his lower lip; he became known as *Big Tom*.

The only thing they had left in the way of gifts was a red and white football jersey and shorts! Tomehu inspected these in silence and then did something that gave the missionaries a start – he scratched their skin with his fingernails because he thought they were wearing paint!

They showed him how to put on the jersey, but he did not like the feel of it against his skin. Willie quickly handed over his bush knife to Tomehu's delight.

Although this encounter was awkward, and perhaps even dangerous, in retrospect the scene was comical, even hilarious; they were standing in the middle of a jungle village surrounded by fierce-looking characters while the chief tried on an Airdrie football strip!

They stayed only one night, then left. It was safer to make the first contact brief, rather than overstay one's welcome.

Every village had its own long house at its heart playing a central role in the community. In the school, which was part of the long house, many learned to read and write and it was good to hear how they could repeat long passages of scripture by heart. At the extreme end of the long house one room was used as a store.

The Indians who hunted, fished and tended the mission plantations had to be paid in kind; there were no money transactions, but large reams of cloth in various colours, fishing tackle, guns for hunting, tools of a wide variety as well as straw hats, sugar, flour and salt were given as payment for services rendered. Salt was an unknown article to the Indian and they thought the taste was so good they would put a lump in their mouths and shout *assucar* which is their word for sugar and quite contrary to the taste of the missionaries! The salt was not refined as we have at home but was in crystal form.

Material would be measured out, perhaps giving enough to make a dress for the Indian's wife. All payment was done in this way. A notebook was kept for the hours of labour done. Each Saturday morning the store was opened and you can imagine these men eagerly awaiting their goods.

Sometimes, however, there were days when some of the Indians just did not want to work.

One day when the men returned from the plantation it was reported to the missionary that one of the Indians had been sleeping instead of working. Naturally the culprit did not like to have his behaviour exposed. However, it was dealt with by the missionary and order restored. Here the missionary had to act many parts, policeman, doctor, teacher to these well-loved Indians.

On another occasion an Indian arrived in the village with a large wound in his back which was caused by an arrow aimed for revenge. Apparently, he had wronged his neighbour's wife. This was just one of the many occasions when Willie's training became essential, since they had studied elementary principles of minor surgery at London's Croydon Hospital. He was able to cope with the situation and dealt with the injury. The word *improvise* is foremost in these situations. All went well and again another golden opportunity was seized to present the Gospel.

First Furlough

The time had come for Willie to go on his first furlough: as he packed he reflected on what had been accomplished during the previous five years.

The missionary is no different from any other servant of God whether at home or abroad; one experiences times of blessing, times of dearth, frustration and disappointment. Reading God's Word and communion with God daily is paramount to equip for missionary service. He gives wisdom to all those who *ASK*.

The day arrived for departure from Indian territory and Willie journeyed downstream to the Mission headquarters in Belem in the State of Para. There were no Aviation Fellowship aeroplanes in those days in the area, so the long journey of two weeks on a small launch turned any reflective mood into one of anticipation to be reunited with parents and all the relatives – not forgetting the Vulcan Street Railway Mission.

He very nearly missed the boat because of wrong information as to its timing. Fortunately, the pilot boat came to his rescue and he journeyed safely home.

Willie looking forlorn as the boat sails without him

Willie's parents were unspeakably happy to have their son return safely home. He had lost so much weight due to the hazards, and a bout of malaria that he had on the boat coming home, that some folks did not recognise him. His mother was soon in control of a good diet for him and so with adequate rest his weight returned to normal quite quickly.

A Welcome Home Social was arranged at the Railway Mission with a large number of interested friends invited. Many of these had been supporting him faithfully through the years he had been in Brazil.

In Glasgow, Willie also received much kindness in many homes including that of a certain Mrs Watson and her daughter Cathie.

You Little Monkey!

Willie had arranged a surprise for his family: he had taken a friend called Kaa-ee back with him from the other side of the world. However, due to the travel arrangements, Kaa-ee arrived in Springburn *before* Willie!

The family were indeed surprised: not only did Kaa-ee arrive unexpectedly – he was a monkey!

Willie had taken him from Brazil in a box, paying the ship's butcher for meat. Monkeys make excellent pets in Brazil, and they can also be eaten; I remember having minced monkey once for a meal. The method of catching a monkey alive is fascinating: prepare a secured jar with a narrow neck containing an attractive substance inside, wait until a monkey puts its paw inside, then walk up and catch it! The monkeys do not wish to let go of the bait, and they cannot remove their paws if they keep hold of it – so they get caught.

Kaa-ee proved to be a magnet to the people of Sprinburn. No-one in the area was unaware of the newly arrived visitor from the jungles of Brazil. He was always active and full of fun – so long as Willie was there to control him. Willie's mother soon discovered how destructive an unhappy monkey can be. Kaa-ee would become lonely while Willie was away on deputation and would demonstrate his loneliness by climbing the curtains of the home; the curtains were not designed for a Brazilian monkey to suspend himself and they were soon pulled down.

Kaa-ee quickly created chaos. The only solution Willie's unhappy mother could find to contain this small bundle of mischief was to lock him in the coal cellar where he could do no harm. From time to time she would throw him hard-boiled eggs, bananas and other pieces of fruit.

Willie was told in no uncertain terms to take the animal to Wilson's Zoo in Oswald Street, Glasgow, and sell it without delay.

Willie & friend

Refuelling – a Feast of Good Things

Missionaries, because of the very nature of their work, are cut off from more experienced Bible preaching, and they suffer a lack of fellowship – isolation can play havoc.

One cannot be giving out all the time without rest and nourishment; refuelling, if you like, for future ministry.

The Keswick Convention in 1939 provided such refuelling. A huge tent was erected to seat a very large audience of people from many Christian denominations, all with a burning desire to know more of God's Word. The message was intended to build up the saints and help them to apply the teaching in their daily lives. For Willie this was a feast of good things.

Deputation

The second half of the furlough had been set aside for Willie to visit churches all over the country, testifying to the way God's hand had been over him.

Complete with Bible, slides and artefacts such as bows and arrows, feather head-dresses beautifully made in gorgeous colours, he began deputation. He travelled all over Scotland and Ireland; at that time there were few cars – Willie carried this bulky and heavy equipment the length and breadth of the land on public transport!

At the time of writing, there are still a number of missionaries on the field who were called to service as a result of his witness. God has wonderfully preserved them with their families.

War had been declared in September 1939 and cities were blacked out at night making deputation hazardous. The warmth of the welcomes, the hospitality received, and the joy of fellowship with God's people were ample rewards for his endeavours.

5. The Power of Prayer

Personal contact with the Almighty is the greatest force
on earth. Philippians 4:6 describes this wonderfully:

> *Be anxious for nothing; but in everything by prayer and
> supplication with thanksgiving let your requests be made
> known unto God.*

My grandfather lived with our family, and my earliest
recollections of him are in prayer. My mother would ask
me to carry a tray through to the sitting room which
Grandpa occupied. As I approached I would hear him
calling upon God, and on entering would see the Family
Bible open on the organ stool. The prayers of mothers,
fathers, grandmothers and grandfathers have far reaching
effects! The latter sentence of James 5:16 says:

> *The effectual fervent prayer of a righteous man availeth
> much.*

Sunday was truly a day set apart for worship. My par-
ents were God fearing and I was brought up accordingly.
Father was an elder in the Henry Drummond Memorial
Church in Possilpark – an office he held for fifty years!

Sunday School

My three brothers and I attended Sunday School at the
Henry Drummond Memorial Church in Possilpark at 3pm.
Then we went to the Gospel Hall which was in a converted
shop in Allison Place off Keppochhill Road, Springburn,
Glasgow, at 5pm. There was no time to be bored then! I
was converted at the Gospel Hall Sunday School when I
was 14 years of age. Never will I forget the faithfulness of
my teacher Miss Anne Stevenson who never failed to re-
mind us of the danger of not responding to the Gospel
invitation.

The Lord had been speaking to me on many occasions
but one particular night on 15th January 1928 after the

lesson, I was truly burdened about my sin and where I would spend eternity. Miss Stevenson opened the Bible and read to me Romans 10:9:

> *If thou shalt confess with thy mouth the Lord Jesus and shalt believe in thine heart that God hath raised Him from the dead, thou shalt be saved.*

She prayed with me and from that moment God opened my eyes and heart to receive Jesus Christ into my life.

My brother James had been converted during an evangelistic campaign in Springburn and he then began attending the Railway Mission in Vulcan Street. When he saw how many young people of his own age attended he invited me to go along too. The wee mission was an ideal place for young people to meet, to learn and to worship.

Encouraging Days

At the mission I found everything that was required to encourage a new convert. I became a member and was soon very involved in tract distribution and open air witness. These were encouraging days.

One couple, Lily and Hugh, returning from the cinema, reflected on how dissatisfying their lives were. On arriving home they found a tract had been put through their door; they read it, saw the invitation to come to the little mission, and on hearing the Gospel were converted. They responded to the faithful preaching, and partook of the Bread of Life.

Lily and Hugh became members, and were dedicated workers; they became the keepers of the hall. What an encouragement this story is to all God's children who are scattering the good seed of the Gospel.

An evangelistic campaign was held by Mr W. P. Nicholson at this time in Springburn Public Hall. Many souls were added to the Mission, and God's blessing was poured upon us.

I remember with affection the wonderful Christian fellowships that were of such help to me as a young Christian, teaching me to read the scriptures systematically and grow in grace. On summer evenings, outings would be organised in the countryside; we held open air meetings and gave out helpful literature. Experiences in the Christian life were shared; there was a real depth of fellowship.

A number of the young people began attending the Bible Training Institute for evening classes. These took place on Mondays and Fridays over four years, at the end of which the student received a diploma. I attended with them and completed the course: it has been of great benefit to me throughout my life.

Nurse Training

I worked in a cousin's shop until I was nineteen years of age. One day, God clearly spoke to me as I worked behind the counter saying that I should seek entrance to nurse training.

In September 1935 my nurse training began. I remember my mother's words to me at that time, she said, "You know it is not just walking up and down the ward in a uniform – you will get some difficult tasks." How right she was! Nevertheless, nothing daunted my enthusiasm and, in spite of my Mum's realism, I took up the challenge.

Having completed Prelim School successfully I was sent as the new probationer to Ward 3A, the Eye Ward, which was part of the general medical unit of Stobhill Hospital, Glasgow. My ward sister had red hair and a temper to go with it. Sometimes I felt she was unfair and harsh with the staff, especially the new probationer!

Soiled linen had to be sluiced by hand before being bagged for the laundry. There were no ready-made sterile packs – we had to make the swabs and cottonwool dabs ourselves, and pack them into a drum that was sterilised in the theatre. The hours were long and with only one day off in the month it was hard going; all for just one pound ten shillings per month!

I remember vividly on my first ward that we admitted a little girl of around nine years of age with pneumonia. Sister called all the nurses to the duty room to inform us of the situation – she warned us that only good nursing would save this child's life. Her threatenings were fearful and we all worked most conscientiously with this little girl, giving heed to all the nursing procedures. I am glad

Nurse Watson

to be able to tell you that she made a good recovery and was able to go home within about two weeks.

Lectures and examinations all had to be done in our own time; I know that life is quite different now in hospital training. I became more and more determined to continue nursing in spite of the hard work; happily, my mother was a good listener, I was able to unload my complaints by talking to her.

A Sacred Experience

I remember being deeply impressed by the reports of a couple from the Mission, Mr and Mrs Kerrigan, who had spent many years in the Belgian Congo, now Zaire. Missionary Committees sprang up which led to the writing and receiving of letters from missionaries. Prayer meetings also sprang up here and there for missionaries. All these activities increased my zeal for missionary work.

During my first year of nursing I became friendly with one of the boys in the Mission, John, who was a qualified masseur. He had studied anatomy and physiology and kindly offered to help in these subjects. The friendship blossomed for about two years.

One night in the prayer meeting at the Mission the Lord spoke to me about this courtship. I had started nursing with one objective, to be a missionary, and here I was on the way to getting married and settling down at home. This young man was a lovely Christian who served the Lord faithfully, but he had not been called to missionary work.

On leaving the prayer meeting I said to John that we would have to part. This was not easy for either of us. We both felt deeply about what was happening, but we both knew that God had his own purpose for us. Looking back on that night, I can truly say that it was a sacred experience.

I went on to finish my SRN training, and completed the first six months of midwifery.

Many Walks

Willie Johnstone had been a friend of my family for a long time. My mother was most hospitable and always encouraged us to bring friends to tea, especially those from the Bible Class. My father was acquainted with a number of young Christian friends who witnessed for the Lord in the Saturday night Tea Meeting. From his conversion, Willie was tenacious in everything, but particularly in preaching the Gospel.

Such tea meetings are not common today. I remember them with great delight, for many hearts were opened by this means to receive the Word of Life.

Willie visited our home on many occasions during his furlough. He had been in fellowship with James, often exchanging good books. I was seldom around during these visits as I was nursing at Stobhill Hospital and on night duty. Our *Paths of Life* had crossed many times over the years – little did I realise that we were to soon join hands on the same path.

One morning when I came home my mother said "There is a letter for you and I think I know who has written it." She had received letters from Brazil during Willie's service there which bore the same handwriting. Retiring to another room to read and digest this very important letter I realised Willie wished to escort me to hospital next day – I was happy to accept! Many such walks ensued!

Willie's furlough was about to end, so he made it clear that he wanted me to be his wife and go back to Brazil with him. I was confident that this was all of God. We were married on 1 March 1940 by Rev Arthur Wallace of Blochairn Church of Scotland, the very minister who had been the means of Willie's conversion!

Since we were not setting up home in Scotland, wedding presents were slightly different. The Mission asked us to put up an equipment list in the vestibule; in this way people would know exactly what we needed: for example, Berkfelt filter, air beds and camping equipment. When I say camping equipment, do not imagine that it was for balmy summer evenings – it was for the jungle, and our beds would be hammocks slung between trees!

Our needs were marvellously provided for.

Cathie & Willie, 1940

New Horizons – My Training for Service

The UFM Council policy for new candidates was to serve two years on the field before getting married. However, there were two reasons for us to be married immediately: single ladies were not allowed to travel alone during war time; and, Willie had five years of strenuous service behind him during which he took part in the traumatic search for the Three Freds; the search had left its mark.

We spent our first weekend after marriage in Balfron with our dear friends the MacKies, already mentioned in connection with the Trekkers; what a lovely Christian home they had. From there we went down to London to meet the Council and make travelling arrangements for Brazil.

On returning to Glasgow, we lived with my parents. Packing began in earnest. A farewell meeting was arranged at the Railway Mission. There was a large gathering and Rev Arthur Wallace left us with a solid foundation from the Word of God. It was the Word and prayer that helped us through many hazards and trials. Such was the kindness shown to us by the Mission and congregation that it will never be forgotten.

6. Brazil Together

Journey to Brazil

We left my parents' home on 9 May 1940, bound for
Liverpool. Emotions were high. Father was standing in the
living room with other members of the family. I shall never
forget my mother's heart-broken state when we walked
into the kitchen. She stood rivetted to the floor, just star-
ing at the cooker in a dazed condition, no doubt thinking
of the dangers of such a voyage in wartime. We kissed her
goodbye, but oh, how it hurt!

Being an only daughter increased the heartache. I have
to confess that tears were in my eyes from Glasgow Central Station until we reached Liverpool. On the next day
we embarked on the ocean liner *Anselm*, which was to be
our home for sixteen days. Due to the war we had to
travel as part of a huge convoy until we reached safer
waters.

It was a Friday when we set sail and on the Sunday we
were attacked by the enemy; we all thought this was the
end. It seemed as though the bottom would fall from the
ship, however, the explosive noises we heard were terrible
depth charges with which we protected ourselves from the
enemy. How we praised God at the preservation of the
vessel and our lives. Life on the boat settled down but the
threat of enemy attack was always present. Every day,
throughout the voyage, lifeboat drills were practised.

The Portuguese meals on board the *Anselm* were my
first introduction to my future diet; it was very different
from Scottish fare. Instead of our usual cereal breakfast,
ladlefulls of stew and vegetables were served. This type of
food is very acceptable at 5pm – but not at 7am!

We had plenty of time for reading and, taking Willie's
advice, I prepared for the study of a new language. Going

through an English grammar book was ideal: I was better prepared by the time my language studies started in earnest in Brazil.

At Lisbon many Portuguese passengers embarked. Everyone was very nervous because of the dangers of the war and one day the Captain asked Willie to give a Word of comfort. He seized the opportunity to preach on Matthew 10:30:

> *But the very hairs of your head are all numbered.*

Our liner finally docked in Brazil around the end of May. The Mission secretary and field leader, Rev Leonard Harris, his wife Doris and a number of other missionaries were there on the quayside to welcome us to Belem, in the state of Para.

Belem Language Study

We eventually arrived at the Mission house in the Rua de Dotre Malcher. Willie set about unpacking – a lot of hard work. He had to unload the less important baggage into the basement, and carry upstairs the things we would need for the future months. My most abiding impression of the first few days are of the abundance of large creepy crawlies, overwhelming heat, an inability to understand the language at public worship and the longing to be able to communicate freely with my neighbours!

From Monday to Friday, language study was the paramount concern, but on Saturday morning there was the camp clean-up. The men would scrub floors and air the rooms, while the ladies dusted and baked.

Each morning, before the duties of the day, we met together for family worship to commit our day to the Lord. The Field Leader would read from the Scriptures and lead in prayer. Each month, one day was set aside for prayer and fasting.

The church building, called the *Cremacao*, was a forty minute walk from the house. We were not able to take the

bus because we had no money for the fare. Often, on returning at night, we were exhausted; rations were limited
and we did not have the luxury of a cup of tea before bed.

For three months, while Willie was on the Gurupi mission station, I shared a room with a beautiful Christian,
Rosemary, who later married Angus Cunningham. We
became good friends and our friendship grew daily: I was
therefore especially saddened when tragedy struck Rosemary and Angus in later years.

I attended Language School for one year at the base
with Mr and Mrs Harris acting as houseparents and secretaries, generally overseeing the well-being of the missionaries.

Whilst I was learning the language, Willie went up to
the Urubu Indian territory to get the house and plantations ready for my arrival.   This involved quite a few
months of separation, but we both had important tasks to
fulfil and got on with it. In all, he was up river for about
three months, and by this time I was making reasonable
progress with the language. On some afternoons I was
asked to visit a few homes, usually of people who were
members of the Christian church. This was excellent language practice and the Brazilians were very tolerant –
even when I made silly remarks!

Visitation

When a reasonable number of more experienced missionaries were at the mission house, this was an oppor-
tune time to visit the prison in Belem. Individual prison-
ers were spoken to and tracts were given to everybody.

There was also time set aside for preaching, singing
and prayer. The good seed of the Gospel was sown, and we
prayed for God's blessing on the visit.

Dia dos Mortos – The Day of the Dead

The Day of the Dead is a day given over to mourning. Mourners clothed in black sit at the graves of their departed loved ones, calling out in an agony of grief, rosary in hand.

This day provided another opportunity for visitation. An open air Gospel meeting would be held, and the missionaries would sit with mourners and seek to give a word of comfort. Oh, the awful despair of those whose trust is not in Jesus Christ who is the only one who gives life and hope!

One day, on returning from visitation, I was delighted to see Willie in the lounge! Due to poor communications he had been unable to let me know that he was returning. I was so overjoyed. However, I had my own surprise for *him* – I was three months pregnant! His visit was short: he had to go back up to the Urubu Indians and would not be back until nearer the time of my delivery.

On another afternoon, while studying in my bedroom situated immediately above the kitchen, there was a very unpleasant odour of fish pie coming up through the floor boards. Times were very bad during the war and sometimes we received no allowances for months, so Mrs Harris naturally had to cut down on the housekeeping. You will recall that Willie was asked what he would do if there were no allowances – this was just such a time. I was actively sick twice, and Mr Harris, a very kind and considerate field leader, asked his wife if I could have a poached egg on toast for once, instead of fish pie. Doris replied resolutely "Indeed she will not – she will just have to get used to the food of the country." Doris was a lovely person, but she knew that I had to acclimatise. She was very highly organised and disciplined herself. Nevertheless, the poached egg on toast came to the table just that once.

At this time Len and Doris Harris had been out in Brazil for nine years without seeing their children. Their

whole ambition in life was to serve Christ. All the fur-
loughs had been knocked out of sequence during the war
years and I think it was another year that they had to wait
before being reunited with their families.

By this time I had satisfactorily completed my study
and examinations, both written and oral. I felt that I had
become reasonably fluent. Willie came back to base from
the Indians, as my time for delivery was now quite near.
We both went out visiting one afternoon to a lady who was
a member of a suburb congregation. I have never forgotten
this visit. Brazilians are very kind and loving people. With
the customary hospitality, a cup of pure black coffee was
soon served. It was the real stuff, but I was not too keen
on it. My hostess said, "Do you like coffee?" I replied that I
did like it, but not in large quantities. Well, that is what I
thought I said—I had actually said that I liked a lot of it,
so she poured out more! I made many mistakes.

In a shop where material was sold for making clothing,
I made a very embarrassing mistake. When I examined
the material in the shop closely, I saw that it was not
really what I wanted—so I said the cloth was good for
nothing! Willie ran out of the shop and I was left with a
red face! Brazilians are really most polite and I am sure
they understood that my vocabulary was anything but
complete.

Short Preaching Tour

From time to time, missionaries who were stationed in
the more isolated places, away from cities and all the conveniences that a city offers, came down river to base in
Belem for some respite.

On one occasion, Mr and Mrs Joe Wright, brother of
martyred Fred Wright, Len and Doris Harris, Willie and I
were all at the base. The decision was made to send Len,
Joe and Willie up the river for a few days on an evangelistic tour.

They visited places in Maranhao and their first meeting was held in Sao Luiz where all the local pastors joined them. The ladies who remained at the base were overjoyed to hear how God had wonderfully spoken to many hearts through the faithful preaching of His servants at the services in this place.

From there they went further up into the interior where UFM had a Bible School. Meetings were held in the open air and large crowds gathered. On one of these occasions a flannelgraph was used depicting the crucifixion of the Messiah and one woman, who was a deaf mute, signalled her desire to follow Christ. Another memorable conversion was that of the organist of the Roman Catholic church in Barra do Corda. That night, when she went home, she was refused entry because she had professed faith in Jesus Christ. She showed signs of growth in her Christian life and finally married one of our national pastors. We met them again after some years and found them still witnessing for Christ.

The men also met with some professing Christians who had become inactive and cold at heart, lacking commitment; they rededicated their lives to God.

When the men returned to Belem we all rejoiced together and praised God for His power being made manifest in the lives of many.

Missionary Service with the Family

Our eldest son Leslie was born on 31 January 1941. I was grateful to Mrs Harris who looked after him at night in order that I might have a proper rest: she did this for all the missionary mothers whenever a child was born at the base.

When Leslie was a few months old, we set out on the long journey to reach the Urubu Indians on the River Gurupi. Having lived in the city of Belem for a whole year I was not used to seeing very primitive scenes. The first part of the journey was by train from Belem to Braganca. The journey took thirteen hours and the departure time was three o'clock in the morning!

This was no express train; it was fuelled by logs of wood which resulted in sparks flying everywhere – on some occasions they would burn holes in the clothing of passengers. The train stopped at every station on the way and vendors went from carriage to carriage selling. They had trays suspended by strips around their necks, displaying their food and drinks.

At one stop there was even time to call at a little house to ask the lady to boil some water for Leslie. She agreed most willingly. Unfortunately, the nappies were soon piling high – no disposable ones then.

On reaching Braganca we were glad to have a meal and refresh ourselves for the second stage of the journey. However, we had scarcely finished when one of the crew from the launch arrived to say that they would be leaving earlier than first planned. Hurriedly we made our way to the launch.

I was horrified by what I saw – a confusing mass of men, women, children and animals. Hammocks were stretched out on two tiers and the confinement was overwhelming. This launch was to be our home for the next thirty-six hours; not only was it grossly over-crowded – there were no toilet facilities!

Vizeu

Arriving at Vizeu we were met by some friends who gave hospitality to Willie in his single days. It was different now that we were a family of three, they could not accommodate us all. They provided us with food, and for accommodation they showed us an old vacant house along the street. There was absolutely nothing in it. The walls had huge gaps in them, but we stretched out our hammocks hoping for some rest.

Two things disturbed our sleep: it was the rainy season and the rain poured in through the roof, so we had to move our hammocks to what we hoped would be a drier position; and, the rats ran up and down the cords of our hammocks! Such circumstances were good preparation for life in the interior, it was the first of many similar homes.

We had to spend a few days in Vizeu to load our own little motor launch the *Boas Novas*. With us also was a new recruit, Frank Winstanley. Willie had arranged for a number of the Indians to bring the launch down from the Gurupi. Purchases were made of food and equipment which would last at least six months. There would be no nearby shops in our village to which we could run for a forgotten item.

Boas Novas

We packed up for a fortnight's journey on the river and set off. We removed the wheels from the pram, and placed Leslie into it; he slept soundly as the motor launch made its way up the river.

The purr of the engine had a soporific effect on him, but the moment it stopped he would cry. At night we slept in the jungle complete with hammock and mosquito net. From time to time we were aroused by the noise of howling monkeys and many other sounds from the animal world. I soon became familiar with the calls of various birds such as macaws, toucans, humming birds, parrots and eagles.

The most hazardous stages of our journey up river was navigating the rapids. Frank Winstanley proved very helpful to Willie in controlling the launch. There were times when we were unable to stop; we could not even make a thirst-quenching cup of tea. Willie would often say to me, "Don't worry, Cath, I know a little village further up and, God willing, we will stop there."

Eventually we arrived, tired and hungry, at a place called Nazareth. Here travellers often dined well; but our expectations were soon dashed to the ground. The fishermen had had no success that day. With pigs grunting around under our hammocks, we lay down that night with only a small cup of the ubiquitous black coffee for sustenance. When we boarded our launch next morning, I prepared something more substantial: Farinha and Quaker Oats – they were always good for a standby meal.

On another occasion, when we had not eaten well, the Indians travelling with us killed a *kotea;* this is similar to a large rabbit with no tail, and has a delicious flavour. We pulled into the bank of the river, kindled a fire, and we had a marvellous barbecue at two o'clock in the morning!

Boa Vista

We finally arrived at the station on the River Gurupi that was accurately named Boa Vista meaning 'beautiful view.'

Overlooking the water was the long house consisting of many rooms. Here we would be staying with our fellow missionaries, plus perhaps six orphans. There were two other rooms which served many purposes, for example – preaching, teaching, clinic and travellers' accomodation.

There was great excitement among the inhabitants who had been listening intently for the sound of our engine purring up river. They were all on the river bank to welcome us, and there was a great deal of curiosity on seeing the first white baby to visit these quarters. As our luggage and equipment were being unloaded from the launch the Indians were desperate to see what was inside the containers.

Due to the fact that we were newly-weds, our kitchen-ware had never been used. As I unpacked a lovely new nest of aluminium pans one forward lady said to me "Why do you have four pans? If you give one to me I will give you this comb," and as she spoke she immediately took the comb from her hair and offered it to me. I explained gently that the pans were a gift from a friend.

This friend, a businessman in the City, had packed a huge tea chest with every conceivable item of equipment for the kitchen and tools for boat building.

We had received many precious gifts on our marriage, beautiful cutlery, teapots and tools of every kind. I was thrilled when I found, on the top layer of all the packaging, a bar of chocolate: Oh, what kindness and love – it was super abundant!

We were closely inspected by the Indians living in Boa Vista and many from other villages who peered into our home – there was little privacy. However, it was wonderful to arrive without mishap and we gave thanks to God for all his protection.

The Long House

There were four missionaries at Boa Vista: Leonard War from Canada who had been there for quite a while, Frank Winstanley, Willie and myself. Life was full as we carried out our respective duties, mine being primarily nursing. I was involved with the school, daily clinic, midwifery and attendance at meetings. Every morning, very early, there was public worship conducted for us all before we took up our daily tasks. Each evening we had Bible studies to end the day.

Life in the jungle is so different to city life. Time has little place in the Indian's thoughts, the tasks of the day fit neatly into place without any reference to clocks: meat has to be salted and put out in the sun; plantations have to be tended, there is fishing to be done and boat building and repair to be organised.

The Congregation

The Indians have a wealth of knowledge about the rainforest; harvesting fruit, fibres and medicine. They practice a shifting cultivation technique called *slash and burn*. They know that the soils of the rainforest are thin and cannot sustain crop growth for more than a few years, so they clear small patches of rainforest, cultivate it for a short time, then move on. They will return from time to time to harvest the area, knowing that trees planted by them will have attracted animals which they can then hunt for food.

The rainforest surrounding the neighbouring Rio Negro has trees which bear beautiful orchids, and one walks on a springy mattress of leaf debris. This debris contains tannin and humic acids which prevents the insects and other micro-organisms from breaking it down; sometimes the mattress is up to three feet deep. Annually, the area averages ten feet of rain, and the tannin and acids are washed out into the river giving it its characteristic jet black colour.

Meeting in the Long House

Plants, fruits, berries, nuts, honey and spices are all taken from the rainforest, together with fish, tapir, wild pigs, rodents, monkeys and birds.

One nut deserves particular mention – the Brazil nut. Brazil nuts are harvested in very hazardous parts of the forest; nut gatherers are attacked by Indians who wish to obtain their tools and firearms.

They are prey to electric eels, fierce piranha, vampire bats, crocodiles, snakes, insects and all the other hungry fauna of the jungle.

The gatherers must wait for the nut to fall; the tree is far too large to climb. What people normally think is the nut, is really just a segment, like the segment in an orange; the nut itself looks like a teapot without a handle, weighs between two to three pounds, and must fall to the ground before it can be harvested. So, another danger is added to an already dangerous living: the falling nuts could kill an unwary gatherer! Spare a thought, then, for those that bring Brazil nuts to your home.

Rainforest plants make essential medicines. Some are used to heal wounds, some as painkillers. Quinine, taken from the bark of the *cinchona* tree, is used to treat malaria. *Curare*, which the Indians use to poison their arrowheads when hunting, is used in surgical operations to relax muscles.

The Brazilian Indians were very numerous at one time. During the 20th century their numbers were drastically reduced because they were being taken into slavery. However, this was not the main reason for the dramatic decline in population: the Indians had no immunity against unfamiliar diseases such as measles, smallpox and influenza. I have witnessed whole villages being wiped out, with the nearest neighbours fleeing to a more distant location for fear of evil spirits.

Rules for Hygiene

One of my patients at the clinic was a little orphan girl, Lily, aged six, who lived in our long house. Her feet were in a dreadful, swollen condition and she was highly fe-

vered. Her condition took a while to cure as sanitation
was bad – they all walked around barefooted exposing
themselves to so much infection. Happily, at that time we
had the drug M&B 693; in the days before Penicillin this
was truly a wonder drug for many of our patients. Lily
improved greatly with this treatment and, of course, she
had to adhere to a new set of rules regarding the protection of her feet!

Willie had told me about the high mortality rate when
he was on the station as a single man. There was much
ignorance concerning hygiene. A woman in the village
professed to be the 'handywoman' which was another

Lily

name for the midwife. I will never forget the first lady I was asked to attend. The house had a mud floor and no furnishings. She was lying in her hammock, wearing the trousers that her husband had worn all day at the plantation. After examining the lady I went back over to my house to prepare a tray for delivery. When I returned to my patient the handywoman was standing in the corner, looking at me with obvious apprehension. I could almost hear her saying, "What is this woman going to do with all *that* stuff?"

On the mud floor lay a big bush knife, normally used to hack a path through the jungle, but for the moment it was to be the tool used to cut the umbilical cord. Small wonder the mortality rate was so high!

My patient was safely delivered of a lovely child; happily, the other women I attended were also safely delivered—though not all so easily as my first patient.

The house where Cathie was midwife for the first time in jungle territory

There was little privacy in the typical Indian village of Brazil. Our dining room was quite open and our view was the jungle. Sometimes we would all be having a meal when perhaps a dozen Indians would walk in and just stare at us without any apology for the intrusion. It was a good opportunity to witness to them—they would remain with us throughout the whole meal.

New Life in Christ

On our station was a lovely Indian couple who had been converted while with us. Their names were Victor and Maria; their faces shone, reflecting the light of the

Victor & Maria

glorious Gospel that was pouring into their once darkened hearts. What a contrast to the sin-scarred faces of those who still lived in fear of evil spirits. Who can deny the power of the Holy Spirit to quicken dead souls to new life in Christ? That couple truly showed signs of growth in grace.

One of the smaller boys in our home was an orphan. His name was Samuel. He was well named because he listened to God's voice and obeyed. He also showed much love and humility in all his duties. He was our house boy and would be up early each morning to start the stove which was fuelled by wood. He did not have matches, but with two sticks he would ignite the wood.

We could cook quite well although the stove was primitive, and the flames surrounded my shining aluminium pots and blackened them. After meals, a number of the boys would take all the pans to the riverside to clean them. There they had a great time.

Victor's Baptism

One day I thought that they were taking a long time so I went down to the river to investigate. I was horrified to see my good pans were being thrown about one to the other in some kind of game. All over the world, boys will be boys!

At Christmas time I so much wanted to make something very special and also to bake, but I had no oven. Frank Winstanley made a wonderful oven for me from two old kerosene tins. It was so heavy that he put it on a pulley so that I could easily manoeuvre it. We had roast duck that Christmas!

I sometimes look back on those days and wonder how we managed. We had no means of keeping food cool. If anything sweet was ever dropped on the table, an army of ants and other insects would have descended on it had the table legs not been standing in tins of creosote.

Sowing the Good Seed

Once a week I had an informal meeting with the village women. This had to be made most simple and it was as

Orphan Boys

though I was speaking to a Sunday School class. Nevertheless, they all listened intently. I cannot say what effect these meetings had on their lives; I simply sowed the seed, perhaps another would reap. We are fully dependent on the Holy Spirit to perform His silent work in the hearts of those to whom we witness.

7. Parnaiba

War

About a year later we received word from mission base in Belem that, due to the war, no missionaries were to stay in unpoliced territory. Sadly, we prepared to leave.

Willie and I were to leave first, Frank and Leonard would follow with the mission property – it was no easy task.

Farewells always have a tinge of sadness no matter where. What can one say? Humanly speaking one wondered why we had to leave those dear people after such a short stay. We are not masters of our own way. I am reminded very much of Jeremiah Chapter 10:23:

> O Lord, I know that the way of man is not in himself: it is not in man that walketh to direct his steps.

We must, therefore, refer ourselves to God and acquiesce to His will.

We packed all the necessary items for a long journey downstream, clothing, food, hammocks, crockery, cutlery. Willie arranged a crew to take us on our way and the pilot was very skilled and knew the river and its dangers very well. We had every confidence in him and above all our trust was in our Heavenly Father who is acquainted with all our ways.

Travelling with us was a man called David who lived further upstream; when a boat is going downstream there is always someone wanting to make good use of the transport.

Journey of Fierce Rapids – and an Inquisitive Child

We had not gone very far when the pilot shouted to us to close all the windows and doors of the launch. He was unable to take us through the usual channel so immediately we found ourselves totally immersed in one of the fiercest rapids; it was a blessing that the motor kept working, we emerged from the rapids safe but soaked. We had taken live chickens with us and they had been washed overboard together with much of our food – the journey ahead would now be even more arduous. We did not have privacy to change into dry clothes, so we sat in the boat letting the tropical sun do its work.

Further downstream we approached a little village. We had been without flour for some time before leaving our station and therefore the thought of buying a loaf was a lovely prospect, so I suggested to Willie that he and David should go and buy some bread. On arrival at the village they set out for the wee bakers shop.

Leslie was sleeping at this time so I thought it would be a good idea to prepare a pudding for him. I lit the primus stove, made the pudding and put it into a bowl, placing it on a bench just at the window to cool. I turned my attention to other things. Meanwhile, Leslie had wakened and toddled along to the pudding. Then, with the usual inquisitiveness of youth—he put his hand into it!

Willie and David had not reached the shop. They heard Leslie scream and came rushing back to the launch. This was a serious accident and there was no chemist. We did not have the necessary first aid kit for a burn of this magnitude. The skin was completely removed from the wrist to the fingertips.

We immediately lifted our hearts to God in prayer that he would send us help to relieve Leslie of this agony. Prayer is a swift messenger which in the twinkling of an eye can go and return with an answer from heaven. Willie cranked the motor immediately and we began to move downstream.

We Prayed – God Heard and Answered!

We had not travelled all that far before we came to a bend in the river. As we turned the bend we saw a Pan American float plane, it had been forced to land due to engine trouble!

Willie asked the Pilot if he had anything to treat burns, he replied, "Yes, I have the very thing in the cabin." It was a large tube of Tannafax. This was a jelly-like substance used in the treatment of burns, which was easy to apply and had no need of a bandage. On application a thick black protective covering soon formed. Now at last Leslie was made comfortable.

The pilot asked us if we were hungry. He brought out tins of corned beef, sausages, a three pound tin of cream crackers and many other goodies we had not seen since we left Scotland. The answer to prayer had been more than we could have thought or asked, not only comfort and healing for Leslie but food for us all.

Philippians 4:19 surely describes how wonderfully God answered our prayer:

> ... *God shall supply all your need according to his riches in glory by Christ Jesus.*

We moored overnight and in the morning, when a relief plane arrived, the controls of the stricken plane were examined and no sign of trouble was found!

God is all powerful, all knowing and we, His children, are dear to His Heart. The outcome may have been very different, but God saw fit to provide medication for Leslie and food for the rest of us in a way that we could not have hoped for, or even dreamed. God answers the prayers of his children according to His Holy Will.

There were a few restive nights ahead with little sleep but glad to say that within two weeks Leslie's hand was completely healed apart from the wrist where there was so much flexion. How thankful we were to our God who is faithful, merciful and gracious.

After many days we reached our Mission base house in Belem. It was so good to see Len and Doris Harris and the other missionaries again. We needed to rest for a bit and be quiet and spend time on the Word and in prayer to seek God's guidance for future service.

During our time of waiting Willie helped in the local churches and we both visited various homes in connection with our little church in Belem city. Mr Harris was a man of great vision who was well aware of the needy places where an entrance to the work of the Gospel was required. I should say that firstly he was a man of God who believed in much prayer and nothing was ever done under his own initiative.

Parnaiba – a Church Planted

Eventually a place called Parnaiba, which is in the state of Piaui, in the north east of Brazil, was suggested as our next field of service. Apparently, missionaries had been there at one time but they did not stay longer than six months. Having committed it to God Willie resolved to visit this town. We understood this city was almost one hundred per cent Roman Catholic – but what a challenge. A city wholly given over to idolatry which Paul speaks about in Acts 17:23:

> For as I passed by, and beheld your devotions, I found an altar with this inscription, TO THE UNKNOWN GOD. Whom therefore ye ignorantly worship, him declare I unto you.

This was the true picture also of Parnaiba, steeped in sin, superstition, fear and ignorance.

On returning to Belem where these findings were again discussed and prayed over, it was then decided that this was the place to preach the Gospel.

We duly left base and went to Sao Luiz in the state of Maranhao to stay with some missionary friends, Mr and Mrs Tom Moses and family. Willie went on ahead to Parnaiba to look for a house. He found one through the instrumentality of one of the bank staff there. Willie returned to Sao Luiz and after a few more days with the Moses family we all set off for Parnaiba. Initially, we stayed for a few days in a small guest house until we could make our house reasonably habitable.

We soon settled into our new routine. The shopping had to be done every day as, just like when we were in the jungle, we had no fridge and there was no way of keeping food cool. I would visit the market every morning at 5.30am! That was the coolest and best time to shop.

There was an abundance of fresh fruit of many varieties. We were told Sunday was the biggest day for the market but that was of no interest to us and on that day we used to have a very light meal, for example, eggs or macaroni which did not deteriorate in the intense heat.

The Growth Begins

We had only been in Parnaiba for a few days when there was a knock at our door. There stood an old lady named Chicinha. I invited her in and she told us that she was a *Crente*, a Christian, and that there was no place of worship in the city. She went on to tell us that she had been praying that God would send a man of God to Parnaiba. Well, our hearts were bubbling with joy as God had answered her prayer and how reassured we were that we were in the right place. She did not stop there but immediately offered us the use of her home; from there we could preach the Gospel.

Her home was in the outskirts where there were no pavements; nothing but sand. The houses here had no furniture, just a big chest in which they kept all their clothes and a hammock which was their bed. There was real poverty.

Chicinha had a son who was very much against Christianity. He used to say to her "Mother, if you will stop being a Christian I will give you all you need." However, she preferred to live simply and to walk and serve her God. In sickness and in health, bad weather or good, nothing deterred this dear soul from the worship of her God.

From her home we had our first meeting. Of course, it was outside the house in the open air as there was no room inside. The climate lends itself well to open air services; crowds gathered and great blessings followed that first witness.

Chicinha

The Church Spreads

Later another old lady appeared, Donna Benedita, from another district in the suburbs called *The Campos*. She offered her home to hold another open air service. This house was situated on the opposite side of the city from where Chicinha lived. Between these two homes the work began and many came to know the Saviour. Do not underestimate what God can do through the faithful witness of two elderly women!

News spread of our arrival. Some called us Scots, others English and some said Americans. No matter what, these names were all mild compared to what had yet to come from the adversary.

Parnaiba is a lovely city, rich materially but spiritually bankrupt. In 1942–43 the population was around 40,000 souls. Its main export was carnauba wax, obtained by beating a palm leaf grown in the area. This wax had several uses, for example, Johnson's Floor Polish, dental substances and the manufacture of lipsticks.

Windmills were a prominent feature in the city as for many homes this was the method of obtaining a supply of water. Being situated on the coast there was always a soft breeze coming in from the sea, aiding the function of the windmills.

We discovered that people moved around quite a bit from place to place, especially in the Northeast when there was drought in the city of Ceara. This of course, influenced the size of our congregation. Many came from Bahia, Ceara and Fortaleza; as in every city, there was a big mixture in the population, rich and very poor. Truly a land of contrasts.

Religious Occasions – or Carnival?

Brazilians love to celebrate every possible occasion. Special saint days are adhered to according to the Roman

Catholic church's calendar and these result in processions with a particular saint lifted shoulder high through the streets with multitudes following.

The Scriptures are clear, in Exodus 20:4 we have the First Commandment:

> *Thou shalt not make unto thee any graven image, or any likeness of any thing that is in heaven above, or that is in the earth beneath ... thou shalt not bow down thyself to them, nor serve them ...*

It is quite startling and thought provoking to see that a carnival can start immediately after such a so-called religious occasion.

Myrddin Thomas & Willie outside our first church in Parnaíba

Dividing the word *carnival* is revealing. The first part of the word *carne* means flesh and second half *vale* means worthwhile in Portuguese. Putting the two together the word literally means that the flesh is worthwhile. The opposite is true for us as Christians because the Scriptures tell us that the flesh is at enmity with God, Romans 8:7:

> *Because the carnal mind is enmity against God: for it is*
> *not subject to the law of God, neither indeed can be.*

To turn from the solemn to revelry in excess so quickly is truly bewildering.

The city square, called *praca* in Brazilian, is the favourite place for walking and meeting people. Night life there is like any other city where much sin is practised. Men love darkness rather than light because their deeds are evil, John 3:19:

> *And this is the condemnation, that light is come into the*
> *world, and men loved darkness rather than light, because*
> *their deeds were evil.*

The congregation in the Campos

Water Supplies

Visitors were usually given a non-alcoholic refreshing glass of *guarana*, this being the favourite drink for most people. A good water supply, however, is a great blessing when it can be obtained. In Parnaiba, donkeys laden with their barrels full of river water would trot around with their vendors from door to door. The water was brown and unsafe to drink without filtering and boiling. Ladies washed their clothes at the river's edge, people bathed and all sorts of filth was deposited in the river. In our home we had two filters. One was a big porous stone suspended on a pedestal with an earthenware water pot beneath. The water from this was still not too safe so we boiled it, let it cool and then transferred it to a Berkfelt filter. Now it was ready for drinking. The candle within the second filter would become so slimy at the end of each week that it needed to be removed, scrubbed and boiled. Missionaries must pay careful attention to hygiene in every aspect, especially in the tropics.

Water in the kitchen tap was only for external use and had to be pumped from a well in our back yard. Willie used to count how many strokes it took to fill the tank.

In the rainy season I collected rain water by putting out a huge basin. On one particular morning, after torrential rain, I went out looking forward to a large supply of fresh clean water – but the basin had been stolen! What a disappointment!

Brazilian Diplomacy

Practically every Brazilian home is furnished with a sewing machine even if there is not another stick of furniture in the place. Most Brazilians are excellent in needlework, which is just as well since in the early days it was not possible to buy a ready-made dress.

I well remember visiting one of my neighbours a few doors down from us who was a highly qualified seamstress. I called on her to ask if she could make me a dress. She was most polite and said readily that she would do so. She took my measurements and told me the amount of material to buy. This I did and took it back to her. "Yes, that is just fine," she said and indicated the date I should return.

So, on the set date, I went back to collect the dress—but she had not even started to make it! She gave me another date to return and the same procedure was repeated. I suggested to her that I would not like to wait too long for the finished article.

She explained that she had been very busy but that she would certainly make it. This seems a very long story about very little but my main reason for telling it is to show that the Brazilian people do not like to say "No" at any time. I remember going home to Willie and saying "surely she is telling lies," but he understood Brazilian diplomacy better than I did.

A Helper for Willie

A student, Abdoral Silva, from the evangelical seminary was sent to help us in the work of the Gospel at this

Abdoral Silva

time. Abdoral met Leonard Harris, our field leader, in quite early days of UFM in Brazil. Len was always seeking opportunities to witness wherever he went and gave this young man a Bible, which for Abdoral was the beginning of great days for him. He continued to read the Bible regularly and became more aware of his lost condition. He realised that nothing could save his soul apart from faith in Jesus Christ who died to save sinners. His whole lifestyle changed and he entered Bible Seminary to equip himself for service to God, wherever He would lead.

He was a very fine student with many qualities that were most commendable to his calling. He was not married and was therefore able to devote all his time and labour to the work. Being Brazilian, he had no language problems. Later, he did marry and served faithfully with one purpose: to promote the Gospel throughout Brazil and other countries. Many churches have been established by him; praise God for national workers who have devoted their whole lives to the spread of the Gospel.

He completed all his studies with much commendation and finally became President of the Alliance in Brazil. This gave him the opportunity to travel far and wide in Brazil in relation to various churches.

Persecution

Early days of residence in Parnaiba were not easy. As the work grew and people were converted, so the persecution began. The new converts readily bought Bibles and were keen to learn more about what God would have them to be. There was a weekly Roman Catholic paper called *Sino* which means Bell in English. This publication printed many false accusations about us. They declared our Bibles were false, but this only increased the desire of our congregation to enquire more closely into God's Word.

On one occasion in the open air, we were surrounded by an organised gang of people led by the priest who threw lemons and eggs at us so that we had to get police protection. We realised that we were truly in a great warfare and could not possibly face the enemy alone. We were reminded of Psalm 115:

> *Not unto us, O Lord, not unto us, but unto thy name give glory ...*

Time was set apart for prayer concerning the great task of making Christ known.

We were always thrilled and encouraged to see new people coming to the services and one Sunday evening a whole family turned up from a suburb called the Tocoons. There was a young man in that family who was deeply moved when he heard Willie preaching on Ecclesiastes 12:1:

> *Remember now thy Creator in the days of thy youth, while the evil days come not, nor the years draw nigh, when thou shalt say, I have no pleasure in them.*

God's Word is quick and powerful and that night that young lad was made aware of the necessity to remember his Creator and to follow in obedience to his commands. I well remember my mother when I was quite young reciting by heart Ecclesiastes 12:13:

> *Let us hear the conclusion of the whole matter: Fear God, and keep his commandments; for this is the whole duty of man.*

This was the best counselling I could ever have had at that juncture of my life. I commend it to anyone who is reading this book, especially to many who think that they are going to enjoy life to the full without taking into consideration their Creator.

War Rages On

During this time war was still raging back home and Willie's youngest brother, Archie, was recruited into the Army. While still in training in the South of England he attended a Salvation Army meeting with another soldier from his unit.

After the meeting a kindly couple invited the two lads home for supper. They remarked on Archie's surname and asked him if he knew of another Johnstone, Willie Johnstone, who had been involved in the search for the Three Freds in 1936. Archie said "I know him well—he's my brother!" Archie carried a picture of Willie, and he had it with him that night.

What a thrilling visit this proved. Who can doubt this clear evidence of God's providential care and leading of His children. Psalm 37:23:

> *The steps of a good man are ordered by the Lord: and*
> *he delighteth in his way.*

God was to call Archie home very soon after this visit— he was killed in action on the Normandy beaches. He was buried in the land where he, and so many other precious souls, fell.

Holidays and Fellowship

Our nearest missionary neighbours were Myrddin and Irene Thomas who lived about 400 miles away in a place called Terezina. They had four children, Geraint, Edwina, Maire and Gwyneth. Fellowship with other missionaries can be a great tonic; the Thomas family would come for a holiday with us whenever they could. Our house was within a thirty minute journey from the beach of Amaracao. One holiday when our families were bathing together young Geraint was painfully stung by a Portuguese Man of War, a jellyfish with venomous tentacles. Thankfully, we were all able to help him and he was soothed and suffered no long-lasting ill effects.

Such times were not all holiday; the last week was always kept for special services in Parnaiba and many gathered to hear the Word of God. It was a time when God's blessing was upon the gatherings. This practice of sharing holidays was continued; we would go to the Thomas family the following year and Willie ministered in their church.

On another occasion Myrddin from Terezina and Leonard Bland from Sao Luiz came to minister. I remember very well talking to Len and saying "I don't really know what I will be able to tell the people when I get home." His immediate response is with me to this day. He said, "Go home and tell the people that you are living for Christ where Satan's seat is." The enemy is ever busy and more especially so when a work of God has just begun. This great enemy is a defeated foe and we know that we are more than conquerors through Him who loves us.

A famous description of Parnaiba was that it was "like a boil that needed to be fomented and fomented with the Word of God." How true this remedy for hardness of hearts proved to be.

Back Row: Willie & Cathie, Irene & Myrddin Thomas
Front Row: Leslie, Gwyneth, Edwina, Geraint

We continued in prayer and preaching in the outskirts of the city where we had several preaching points. The congregation grew and we felt that it would be good to get premises in the centre of the city. We were hindered by the priest on many occasions when we thought that we had secured a place for worship. Finally, we were allocated a small hall near the main square.

Despite ridicule, the Word of God was reaching the people and many professed faith in Jesus Christ. One of the new converts, a joiner to trade, offered to make all the seating for the new church – he made an excellent job, and out of best quality wood. Our hearts were full of gratitude to God for sending this gifted man into our congregation and using his skills for the Lord's house.

After nearly five years in Parnaiba there was a congregation of around forty; and so the Word of God was firmly established there. At the time of writing, a church now stands; built on the spot of our original very small premises.

Back Row: Willie & Myrddin
Front Row: Cathie with Leslie, Edwina,
Irene Thomas with Gwyneth, Geraint

Now Brazilians are very fond of children and we found that we gained an entrance into many homes because of Leslie. This was a great blessing but he caused us times of anxiety too. On one occasion he became ill with a very high temperature. The doctor treated him for malaria but to no avail. I asked the doctor's permission to give him M&B tablets that I had in the house. He had deteriorated rapidly and when permission was granted for the tablets to be given, immediately the temperature came down. He was diagnosed later as having had pyelitis.

Another time of anxiety was when he was bitten by a dog as we walked together in the street. The appropriate

Leslie

injections were not to hand so an SOS was sent to Myrddin Thomas in Terezina, who promptly sent the injections by the next plane. All turned out well with no ill effects from the bite. We are thankful to God for the good health we enjoyed despite being exposed to so much disease.

The British Consulate, Mr Smith, was friendly and kind toward us and would invite us now and again to dine or have a coffee with him. When the Thomas family came to Parnaiba for a holiday, Mr Smith very kindly offered his beach house at Aramacao to us for

a month. This was just marvellous, and it was secluded; there was no house within a radius of about two miles.

What about our supplies? The Consulate arranged for a lad to bring our stores daily!

This seclusion would not suit everyone, but I was now six months pregnant with our second son, Donald, and I was specially thankful that we were not on the packed beaches of Rio de Janeiro. We thoroughly enjoyed the tranquillity and fellowship with our dear friends; the children were happy and contented – another bonus!

This pregnancy ended in a normal delivery in a modern Roman Catholic hospital in Parnaiba which was mainly staffed by nuns. Although they knew why I was in Brazil our religious differences did not minimise their nursing care and attention.

As I write these experiences I am reminded so much of our world today with all its bustle and never-ending expression of 'No Time.' Everyone in Christian service needs seasons of quiet reflection.

The following hymn by William Dunn Longstaff (1822–1894) helps express my thoughts. We used to sing it in the Christian Endeavour so many years ago.

Leslie & Donald

> *Take time to be Holy*
> *Speak oft with thy Lord*
> *Abide in Him always and feed on His Word*
> *Make friends of God's children*
> *Help those who are weak*
> *Forgetting in nothing His blessing to seek*

Take time to be Holy
The world rushes on
Spend much time in secret with Jesus alone
By looking to Jesus
Like Him thou shalt be
Thy friends, in thy conduct, His likeness shall see.

Take time to be Holy
Let Him be thy guide
And run not before Him whatever betide.
In joy or in sorrow,
Still follow thy Lord
And looking to Jesus still trust in His Word.

Take time to be Holy
Be calm in thy soul
Each thought and each temper beneath His control
Thus led by His Sprit
And filled with His love
Thou soon shall be fitted for service above.

Tragedy Strikes

The time had come for my old room-mate Rosemary's
darkest hour: she and Angus planned a five-day journey
up the river Xingu from Altamira to take the Gospel to
Brazilian Indians. They were to be accompanied by their
three-year-old son, Robbie. Angus wrote to his friend Horace Banner on 22 February 1946:

> "It seems hard for me to even write about the news of
> our precious Robbie's departure but I know you will want
> to know just how it happened. It was a Saturday, three
> weeks ago, and we boarded the Dois de Julio about
> 4.30pm. There were only three other passengers beside
> Leonido and the crew and two of the passengers were to
> get off about midnight and so we had all the accommoda-
> tion we could wish for under the circumstances and it
> looked as if we were to make one of the best trips ever –
> five days and nights. Our loving Robbie was so happy to
> at last be on his way up to the Indians. He was just
> thrilled as he stood up with us at the prow of the launch
> and then sat on our knees and asked questions. He had

anticipated the trip so much and on the last day could not take his nap at midday because he was so excited and just stayed awake singing and talking. He told me often that he wanted to tell the Indian boys about Jesus.

We sat down to supper at 8pm and Robbie was getting sleepy and ate little. When we got up from eating I washed both Robbie's and my hands and then told Rosemary to wash her hands whilst I took Robbie and got him ready for his hammock. Mrs New Year's oldest girl Nene was with us as we had asked if she could come along to help with Robbie and be company for Rosemary. I sat Robbie on the floor while I reached behind the mosquito net (both Robbie's and his Mommie's hammocks being tied together and the mosquito nets being in place around them) to get his things which were on top of one of our trunks. Robbie was sitting on the floor almost against my leg and as soon as I had what I needed I turned around and just at that moment Nene came up from behind and asked where Robbie was, because she had seen him just a second before sitting on the floor beside my leg. I told her he was here but looking down couldn't see him and began searching under the hammocks and nets for him. Then she said she heard something fall in the river but I couldn't believe it was he and called and searched some more around our sleeping quarters. Leonido was in charge of the launch and heard me call Robbie. He also said he thought he had heard something fall in the river. Oh Horace, you cannot imagine the horror of that moment. I ran to the back of the launch to jump in the water but it was as dark as pitch. The launch was already turning and I had my pants and shoes off ready to jump but they told me not to as it would only make another one to hunt for and would mean less possibility of finding Robbie. The launch turned back down river with the bright lights at the front to aid us. I had just fitted them myself before we set off. We never dreamed for a moment that we would not see Robbie's dear head and pull him out from the water. We went up and down and up and down but all to no avail. Oh, the horror of those moments. Only the hand of God could have sustained us. We cannot doubt but that God took him, but it was so hard to think of our little one going like that. No one even saw him and he never uttered a word. It was in an instant. Even after washing her hands Rosemary said she was about to come to us but something seemed to refrain her and persuade her to tarry and wash her face too. It could only have been, Horace, that God willed to take him home in that manner. Yes, he has given his precious life for the Xingu people.

Leonido suggested that we come right back and he asked all the neighbourhood to make a thorough search of the river the following day. And so we came back to Altamira arriving at midnight. You can imagine our heartache to come into this house without our precious boy who was our joy. I must admit, Horace, that all the people did everything to comfort and console us, even those who seemed to be bitter enemies of the Gospel. Isa and Isomar were Roman Catholics and hostile to our church but they became like sisters to Rosemary and insisted that we go over to their house where we spent two weeks. May God reward them and also grant them the salvation of their souls.

For the next eight days launches went up and down searching for the body of our darling but no results. On the eighth day his body was found at the rivers edge. It appears that his body went right down to the bottom and his little foot got caught in some creepers at the bottom of the river where only after eight days he came to the top with his little foot missing. His body was brought here on Sunday morning and the burial service was held immediately.

Since the above was written Mariana has arrived and has given us your kind letter written just before your departure. Thank you so much, Horace. Your words are such a comfort to us and I know that you, along with many others have prayed so faithfully for us during this dark hour of our affliction. You will never know what a comfort your telegram was to us. God bless you. As yet we are undecided as to when we will go up-river. I want to make a short trip, maybe down-river, or perhaps we might even go to the Iriri. This is just speculation as we are looking to the Lord to guide us. The dentist's two sons have taken a stand for Christ and also Chico and Luiza,

Ilias' daughter. Two other smaller boys stood up in the Young People's meeting but I cannot say that they understand fully, although they did both pray as we dealt with them afterwards. How we long to see the Spirit of God really at work in the hearts of the people here. Let us pray that a conviction of sin might really come upon them. How we are looking forward to seeing the Indians! I hope it will not be too long before we see them again. Must close for now. Rosemary joins in sending our love and greetings. Your loving brother in Christ – Angus."

8. Deputation

After seven years our term on the field was coming to an end and we began looking forward to furlough and being with our loved ones again. We boarded a cargo ship with a crew of twelve in April 1947; as we were the only passengers, we were invited to dine with the Captain and crew for each meal.

The food and service were top class and, as the voyage lasted a whole month, we delighted in the restful time and managed to put on a little weight.

Great care was needed on the voyage home as Leslie was only six years of age and Donald three – with all their eagerness to run around and see all that was going on downstairs, they needed constant supervision.

As the day was fast approaching for landing, again we were overpowered with emotion at the very thought of being reunited with our families and friends. Also, the grandparents were keenly looking forward to seeing their grandchildren for the first time.

We were welcomed home by members of the London Council and following a meal we boarded a train at Euston Station for Glasgow. At Central station some members from our families were eagerly waiting for us. It was May but the weather was exceptionally cold—and our clothing was designed for tropical conditions!

When we arrived at my parents' home in Walnut Road, Springburn, there was a splendid fire burning brightly. Our children were amazed; they had never seen a fire like this. Their faces were truly a study and they appreciated the fire's warmth. Houses in Scotland are so different in their furnishings to those in a tropical climate where everything is planned for coolness.

Leslie and Donald spoke only Portuguese for a few weeks. Even when out playing with Glasgow boys at football, they babbled away. However, they soon started to speak English which was just as well since Leslie had to start going to the school which was near my mother's home.

My parents made us as comfortable as their limited accommodation allowed. Here we would make our home for at least a year – or so we thought.

Before setting off for Scotland we had visited a Children's Home in Fortalenza to make arrangements for the children's schooling on our return to Brazil. The Home, together with a school, was owned by the Mission and run by Mrs Eva Mills. However, during our furlough, this establishment was closed down and we were faced with a whole new situation to consider.

New Field of Service – Deputation Secretary

These post-war years were difficult with regard to vision and mission; wide representation of the Mission was obviously needed. Three experienced missionaries were home from Brazil on furlough, Len Harris in London, Joe Wright in Belfast and Willie in Glasgow. Prayers were uttered in many quarters, at UFM, the home churches and privately; prayers for guidance as to the future of UFM and individual lives.

The Council summoned Len, Joe and Willie to a meeting at headquarters in London. They all had years of experience on the mission field, and were tenacious in everything they put their hands to, therefore the Council asked them to represent the mission at home as Deputation Secretaries.

After considering the change of role prayerfully, they all accepted their new tasks. Mr Harris became the Mission's representative in the London area, and then went on to become General Secretary. Joe Wright and Willie became the Mission's representatives in Ireland and Scotland, respectively. Miss Bird, a faithful servant to her

God and to the Mission, had recently retired from being Deputation Secretary for UFM in Scotland and Ireland.

During Willie's first furlough he had to travel on public transport; he found himself doing so again for a time until the work became established. Deputation involved a great deal of travel and separation from family for weeks on end. It involved visiting churches and mission halls as far away as Wick and Thurso, the Orkney and Shetland Isles, the Western Isles and the Borders; however, apart from the strain of being parted from the family, it was a time of blessing and a time to make new friends!

The days of deputation were difficult. Having so much equipment to carry for the work Willie was restricted to a very small amount of changes of clothing. I used to send parcels of clean clothes, and other necessities, on ahead for him. Willie just loved the work and God blessed in many quarters. Having been the recipient of so much lovely hospitality Willie would say to people "Now if you are ever in Glasgow do come and visit us," and sometimes they did.

One afternoon, about three o'clock, the telephone rang. Two ladies asked if they could drop by for a visit. Willie was out of town on deputation, and the house was in disarray, but it was lovely to have them for tea; we renewed our fellowship in the Lord. The ladies had opened their homes for prayer meetings for missionaries over many years. Over a meal, we spent hours talking about what God had done, and was continuing to do.

One of our elders, Evan MacDonald, reflecting on his childhood in the North of Scotland, still comments on those early years when bows, arrows and feathers fascinated young and old alike. The biblical precedent for missionary deputation meetings is in Acts 14:26-28 where the Apostle Paul reported what God had done:

> *And thence sailed to Antioch, from whence they had been recommended to the grace of God for the work which they fulfilled.*

> *And when they were come, and had gathered the church together, they rehearsed all that God had done with them, and how he had opened the door of faith unto the Gentiles.*
>
> *And there they abode long time with the disciples.*

What a lot they had to say. Souls saved, churches opened, lives preserved, fellowship deepened. How good it is to be thankful like the Apostles and relay to the church all that God has done.

Those days were difficult in many ways because of our young family causing us apprehension; nevertheless we were happy knowing that this was the way that God wanted us to go. I was expecting another child and so we moved in with Willie's parents; we had two rooms to ourselves.

Our third son, Christie, was born 25 December 1948, and our only daughter, Heather, was born fourteen months later. The accommodation was confined now with six of us between two rooms.

We shared the kitchen with my mother-in-law; fortunately she was easy to get on with. There was one snag – she had a lodger who slept in the dining room near the kitchen!

At night I tiptoed through to the kitchen to prepare a feed for the baby; the more I tried to be quiet the more noisy and clumsy I became. One night I dropped a pan, full of milk, onto the floor just as I was about to put it onto the cooker. The lodger was not amused – but then neither was I!

This gives you a little insight into what it meant to be sharing in such a small home. However, that phase passed and as I look back now I realise that it was all working together for our good.

Many of God's people north, south, east and west opened their homes for the reading of missionary letters and prayer. These were the people who were standing by the staff and to this day we are grateful to God for raising up such people. Local secretaries assisted in organising venues where the Deputation Secretary could conduct a series of meetings. One such secretary was Mrs McKenzie of Inverness; she laboured tirelessly for over forty years and gave hospitality to Willie during his travels.

One Fife businessman provided support for missionaries by paying for the purchase of the Maranatha river launch.

In the Winter months travelling was arduous, especially in the Highlands when snowdrifts frequently made roads impassable. There were many kind families who always said to Willie, "When you finish your tour in the North bring Cathie to have a wee holiday." We experienced memorable times of God's great kindness through His servants far and near. Hospitality is a wonderful word. Many saints throughout the country showed us so much kindness.

Around April the tour of the North finished and Willie would then take our three sons into the country. Leslie became a keen bird photographer as a result of those days.

As our boys grew older Les and Donald would accompany their Dad to services, helping him with the equipment. By this time we had a Ford Popular car which was a wonderful aid for the work.

One wintry night fog came down making their journey very dangerous. It was getting late and I was beginning to get anxious. The phone rang; it was Willie to say that they would be late – the fog had worsened and it was now frosty. The car had no heater and their breath clouded the windscreen; this, coupled with the keen frost, reduced visibility to nil. Late they were—but they eventually made it home safely.

Annual Meetings and Conferences

Annual meetings were important dates on the calendar and Willie would invite the platform party to tea; a special joy to us both. Meetings were well attended in those years and I can well remember the BTI lady students sitting in the front row wearing their little black bonnets – uniform style. Many were influenced by seeing the slides and films, and heard God's voice calling them to service.

Weekend conferences were started; the first one was held at Laurel's Guest House, Rothesay, with around 20 people attending. Our numbers increased as time progressed. Other conferences were held at the Balvonie Conference Centre in Skelmorlie on the Clyde coast, Seaside Heights, Netherhall, and in Bonskeid, Pitlochry. The Bible readings were most edifying and our vision enlarged as we listened to reports from the various Mission fields.

As the work grew it became necessary to find an office in Glasgow. Through the help of a Christian friend we acquired a room on the top floor at 280 St Vincent Street, Glasgow – the Scripture Union headquarters. The Lord graciously supplied helpers too. Mr W. Kater was a retired Christian gentleman who offered his services to help Willie in the office and gave faithful service. Marion Small worked with Willie for many years and was a great organiser for the conferences. Andrew, her husband, was faithful in leading the prayer meetings in the home of the MacKenzie ladies at Ibrox. We were so grateful to these dear ladies for their kindness; they were five sisters and their home remained dedicated for prayer and hospitality for at least sixty years! How comforting to know that one day all those seemingly quiet services will be made known. Encouragement is given to us in Ecclesiastes 9:11:

> *...the race is not to the swift, nor the battle to the strong, ...*

At the time of writing, the Scottish Secretary for UFM is Andrew Ballantyne; he was also leader of the Ibrox prayer meeting for many years. Bert Clark is now Chairman of the Scottish Committee, and we had a most proficient secretary in Lily MacKay until she passed into Glory. Lily was appointed office Secretary after Mrs Small retired in 1984. She was proficient in every avenue of her duties, and sensitive to people's needs when illness or tragedy struck. Every visitor to the office was welcomed with a loving smile, and a refreshing cuppa!

In October 1994, Lily and a lifelong friend, Mrs Tweedie, visited Lily's sister in Indianapolis, America, for a holiday. Their return flight ended tragically when the plane crashed in Chicago – every one on board died. With such a stark reminder of the brevity of life, we should prepare our hearts for eternity; Lily and her friend had made that preparation many years previously. We continue to uphold in prayer all the relatives and friends of those two saints in the Lord.

Holidays

For about seven years in succession we went to St Monans for a holiday. I will never forget our first visit there. Leslie was ten, Donald seven, Christie seventeen months and Heather only three months old. The house had been recommended to us by a friend. The accommodation comprised one room containing three beds and a cot, and a kitchen.

To begin with we were uncertain and a little apprehensive about the whole thing, but now looking back over the years it turned out to be one of our very best holidays.

We arrived at St Monans railway station, got off the train and trooped down the road to the holiday house. We found our landlady sitting outside in the garden awaiting our arrival. She exclaimed, "A' didnae ken that ye had such a sma' wean!"

She was a great landlady and the house was sufficient for our needs. We stayed there for a month for £8; can you wonder that we went there for seven years in succession! Willie took the boys out each morning; when they returned dinner was waiting. After dinner the family washed the dishes and were all out again by 2pm. The weather throughout that whole month was glorious.

It is lovely now to reflect on those days when Heather was only a toddler. I remember her Dad would lift her shoulder high along the little narrow streets with high walls and she would pick a flower here and there.

Holidays in St Monans

During one visit to St Monans we met Mr and Mrs Elliot who were also on holiday. We had children's meetings at the beach mornings and evenings; Mary Elliot was expert at speaking to the children using Flannelgraph and figures on the blackboard. They were a great help to us. In the evenings, football was arranged for the boys and open air meetings were held at the harbour. We were encouraged by the many lovely Christians who rallied around us.

We have fond memories of two lovely holidays in the North at Bettyhill and Helmsdale when our children were quite young. The churches there were in vacancy so Willie was invited to come, with family, to holiday in one of the manses and to take the services. This kindness shows God's provision for us as a family, to enable us to have these holidays, and also His provision of care for His flock in the area.

The manses were empty of all furnishings, so the kind members of the congregation supplied the necessary furniture and all the basic necessities of a home for us to use. They even provided a supply of peat for the fires, every last need was met – how devoted those saints were!

Willie Returns Briefly to Belem

Between January and March 1962 Willie returned to Brazil. He had been invited to give the Bible readings to our missionaries at their annual conference in Belem; this is a time of great blessing for them when they all congregate at the Mission base. Some travel many miles for this very special occasion. Fellowship is renewed among missionaries and some parents are reunited with their children—it is altogether a wonderful time.

Missionaries become exhausted physically, and also spiritually, after continually pouring all their energy into the work; they need to be refreshed and spiritually fed to enable them to minister effectively to their churches when they return to their respective stations.

I was unable to accompany Willie; Heather was still only twelve. One day, just before Willie left, we met a lady in town. She asked me if I was going too; when I said that I would be staying behind, she encouraged me by saying, "Well, Cathie, that will be your contribution to the Lord's work." I was deeply impressed and that comment brought me great comfort during future separations.

Willie arrived in Recife in the early hours of a Friday morning. His itinerary had been arranged by Rev. Ted Laskowski; it covered the whole missionary field and gave Willie the opportunity to visit every single missionary on the job.

Willie gave a short address at the Presbyterian Boarding School in Recife, then left for Belem, arriving after nightfall.

On Sunday he spoke at the Marituba Leper Colony, then later took the services at the mission church. In the early hours of Monday morning Willie travelled by MAF plane to the MAF base at Araguacema, then went on by plane to Gorotire on the Xingu.

By the end of his first week back in Brazil, Willie had visited all the Indian work on the Xingu, had taken five hundred feet of film, and was back in Belem!

There followed many trips up the Amazon, visiting the bases of the three Amazon launches and many churches in the area. An extensive tour was made of Maranhao State, the highlights of which were the Christian Workers Conference in Sao Luiz and the Colinas Convention. At Colinas, new converts were made and recent converts were baptised.

Willie departed Colinas by MAF plane and arrived in Teresina, Piaui, in just over an hour. Here he was uplifted by Wesley Gould and taken by jeep to Piracuruca. After a weekend conference there, and visits to outlying districts, a week was spent in Parnaiba. Great changes had come over Piaui; a day of evangelism had dawned on what had been one of the hardest parts of the field.

The visit ended with brief visits to Remanso, in Bahia, and Maceio, in Alagoas. It had been rather hectic but souls were saved, backsliders were restored and believers were blessed.

Willie compiled a report of his experiences and observations; he delivered this to a UFM council meeting on 15 October 1962. He remarked that when he had left Brazil many years before with his family, the Alliance had been only a name; by 1962 it had embraced almost forty churches and congregations, and had thousands of members. Also, in 1962, the Alliance had for the first time appointed a President who was a national, Abdoral Silva, who had been Willie's helper in Parnaiba – a wonderful sequel to Willie's teaching and training.

Fellowship and Worship

Willie was away preaching most weekends. Our local church, Springburn Baptist Church, was within walking distance from our home in Balornock; I attended this church regularly and the children were active in various organisations. I had an amusing experience one Sunday morning following the service when a lady turned round to speak to me and said, "Oh my, I see you have four children. You must have had it hard to bring them up without a man!" She thought I was a widow.

Willie preached regularly at Lambhill Evangelical Church and we, as a family, enjoyed good fellowship with the people there. There were a good number of young people in the congregation and our boys met lots of people their own age. One Sunday after lunch the boys asked me if they could invite some of the young ones up for supper and I asked how many they thought would come. The reply indicated perhaps a dozen and I will never forget my amazement as car load after car load arrived bringing forty people! They all thoroughly enjoyed being together; it is good to encourage our children to bring their friends home, especially in Christian circles. Bible Training Institute students would also call in often for tea and have fellowship with us.

Willie and I loved to have missionaries stay with us even if it was just for a night. Our accommodation was very limited, but the floor was good for the overflow!

Joe and Mamie Wright from Ireland, stayed with us for a fortnight on one occasion. Lily Heath came every year for a fortnight; she was a delight to have. Len and Doris Harris too were always welcome guests; the McAllisters, missionaries in Zaire with UFM, would use the house when we went away on holiday.

The Brooks family lived in Kirkcaldy and were active members in the Gospel Union there where Willie used to preach regularly. Mr Brooks once suggested that we could exchange houses as they would like to come to Glasgow for a holiday; we welcomed this idea and enjoyed a lovely holiday at their house overlooking the sea.

While staying in the Brooks' house we were invited to tea by two ladies who were members in the Gospel Union Hall; the boys were horrified – the day was a scorcher and they wanted to stay outside and play football. They thought that they would be bored to tears. The table was laden with goodies and the children had fun trying to spoon sugar and cut cakes. After tea, we all went into the sitting room in which there were toys and an organ. Despite their fears the children were overwhelmed by the warmth and generosity of the ladies and had a thoroughly good time.

These are just a few of the many lovely times we enjoyed with God's people.

A Change of Fellowship

Through time, in God's providence, we joined St Vincent Street Free Church of Scotland, in Glasgow; Rev A. G. Ross was the minister. We were warmly welcomed by all. Willie became an elder in the church in 1972. George Gilgis, Heather's husband, was made a deacon at the same time as Willie was made an elder, and Heather taught in the Sunday School. How we appreciated the expository preaching and God's sovereignty being made known. Willie was away a lot on deputation but when possible sought to help in the congregation.

Around that time the Women's Foreign Missionary Association meetings were held in the home of the late Bessie Cook in Woodlands Drive. Numbers were small but we had lovely times of fellowship. We learned the latest news from the mission fields, and laid our petitions for the work before the Lord. May Robertson was another of those very dedicated ladies who served the Lord for more years than I can recall. Mrs Ann MacDonald joined us at these small gatherings and made a great contribution; she is still extremely active in all the work of the church.

In 1972, Rev Ross accepted a call from Oban Free Church and about eighteen months later, in 1974, Rev Douglas MacMillan was inducted to St Vincent Street Free Church from Aberdeen.

Bishopbriggs Prayer Group

One night, as we were leaving the house for the evening service, an inner voice spoke to me saying, "Yes, you are getting plenty of spiritual feeding, but what about the neighbours around you who don't attend church?"

I made my inner feelings known to my neighbours, Mrs Myers, Mrs Jones, Mrs Chalmers and Mrs Hamilton, Christian ladies actively engaged in their churches. All of them shared the same concern for others. Rev and Mrs Jones, and a number of others from their congregation, were very enthusiastic about this witness.

We met for prayer and discussed how we should plan and put into action our desire. God controls our thinking and I believe that what is truly of God is ordered by him; there is always someone or some place appointed for the fulfilment of what God has first initiated.

We met for prayer on the Tuesday preceding the Sunday fixed for the meetings. The meetings began at 8pm on the Sundays; by then most church services were over.

Speakers would be invited to speak on various topics to as many as were willing to come. Quite a good number would gather and showed great interest; the Gospel was faithfully preached.

Bible-based Teaching

Mr Morrison, Rector of Graeme High School, Falkirk, spoke on one occasion on the subject *"What is a Christian?"* He said that contrary to popular opinion Christianity is not a matter of biology or heredity. He defined a Christian as someone who believes in Jesus Christ, a personal belief involving the heart and soul. He said that to the Christian, Christ's death is seen as essentially purposeful, significant as God's way of dealing with human weakness—sin.

One Sunday we discussed the relevance of the Bible in an increasingly complex and troublefraught society. The speaker, Jack Campbell, a young Glasgow teacher, proved ably equipped to deal with this searching topic: he believed the power of the Christian Gospel, and he had firsthand experience with problem children who lead fundamentally aimless and unrewarding lives.

From chapter two of Mark's Gospel, Mr Campbell showed how Jesus heals a man's spiritual needs first, then he can function usefully in society. We discussed how social work had mushroomed in an effort to save society; it was agreed that the Biblical order of individual, then social structure, was not only logical but irrefutable. How can the Bible be dead if it has the power to make men alive?

"What the Bible means today." Dr. George Chalmers, a Glasgow geriatric consultant, approached this broad subject by speaking authoritatively from his vast knowledge of elderly people and their problems. He stressed the very real need for, and blessings of, the Christian faith in the twilight years of life.

Basing his talk on Ecclesiastes chapter 12, he spoke of how old age is generally regarded as the embodiment of the meaninglessness of life. Eventually we all grow old, life loses its freshness and appeal; nothing is new any more; there is physical decline, appalling loneliness, and above all, fear.

However, Dr Chalmers rejoiced to be able to testify from personal experience that God gives saving health to young and old alike! Nicodemus, on asking how a man could be born when he was old, was told:

> For God so loved the world that he gave his only begotten son, that **whosoever** believeth in Him should not perish, but have everlasting life.

Many years later I met a lady at the local shops who had been faithful in joining with us. She said, "You will never know how much I was helped and encouraged in my faith at those meetings." Nothing is in vain when we labour for the Lord in His Name.

9. Return to Brazil – 1973

The Quest for Eldorado

The River Amazon flows in an easterly direction and virtually bisects the tropical rain forest region of Northern Brazil. The Xingu, one of the principal tributaries of the Amazon, is 1,230 miles long, and flows into the Amazon at Porto da Mos from the south. The upper course of the river lies within the state of Matto Grosso and within the southern segment of the state of Para for the various streams within the northern part of the plateau of Matto Grosso merge to form the Xingu River.

Today, Altamira is on the Trans-Amazonian Highway which was cut through the rain forest south of the Amazon in 1970–73. Towns on the tributaries south of the Amazon are linked by this highway; for example, Altamira on the Xingu is linked to Itaituba on the Tapajos, a southern tributary of the Amazon to the west of the Xingu.

The following is an excerpt from a Horace Banner Prayer Letter, from 1971, entitled *Quest for Eldorado*.

Eldorado – the fabulous "golden land" which inspired the Spaniards in their conquest of Mexico and Peru and which cost Sir Walter Raleigh his head, when he failed to bring back from Guyana a shipload of Gold for King James 1st. Today the quest is on in Brazil, it began in September, right here in Altimira on the Xingu river where this page is being written, when a start was made on the Trans-Amazonian Highway. Donna Eva and I have come down here to see things for ourselves instead of flying direct from Smoke Falls to Belem for our annual missionary conference.

Giant bulldozers and men with the last word in forest clearing equipment are driving East and West towards targets 2,500 miles apart. Ahead of the machines go selected Indians in the hope of avoiding conflict with tribes whose hunting grounds are now being so rudely invaded. Among the trail blazers are some of the trusted Kayapos.

Of course, what the master planners have in mind are not so much treasure cities, lost civilisations or the remains of prehistoric monsters, but the minerals which in this atomic age are more precious than mere gold. By the time the Highway is completed the Amazon rain forests will no longer hold any secrets. Hitherto untapped resources will be available and living space provided for thousands of bold frontiersmen and their families.

In Altamira the Indian trail blazers come in to spend their wages. Amid such an array of shops, paint and parrot feathers have lost their appeal. Imagine never having even seen big money before and suddenly finding yourself with seventy pounds to spend. No use telling them to save, for there are no shops in their villages and in Brazil inflation is such that money needs to be turned into goods in a hurry since it shrinks overnight! So the Indians have bought good clothes, mosquito nets, blankets, hammocks, perfume, toys, dress-lengths, powerful flash lamps, leather suit cases, wedding rings and some gold teeth – as if their smiles are not bright enough! Extravagant? Maybe, but for all that, their careful spending has become the talk of the time. While some of the other tribes are crazy for drink and the wild life of this modern Klondyke, our Kayapo Jesus hearers have steered clear of the saloons and pimps, night clubs and even tobacco. They are as well known in the churches as in the shops.

Brazilian Christians (as at home, men are greatly outnumbered) have turned in their seats as our 14 smart young men have walked in alongside Dad and Mum! Though unable to understand much of what the preachers say they are always ready to stand up, sing and pray in their own language, when invited, and in our chalet home we have often seen these 14 heads bowed low in prayer as they have remembered their loved ones at Smoke Falls and Gorotire.

Now with their spearhead work done they are heading back home with their purchases. The machines drive on in their efforts to transform the Amazon Rain forest into Brazil's golden land. We are vitally interested in the new highway, but for its people rather than its other so-called treasures. We want to see more of God's "Golden Ones" made from the likes of these Kayapos who, to use their own expression have "made Jesus their own."

1973 marked the fortieth year of service in the Mission for Willie; he was invited to go to Brazil again to minister to the missionaries. The invitation came from our Council in London to attend the Annual Missionary Conference in Belem and then to minister at the amazon Valley Academy for missionary children. He would be ministering to all who gathered for encouragement in the work.

This time I was able to take leave of absence from my work and could accompany Willie; we were delighted! Our four children had now grown up and were all married.

Scottish Winter to Brazilian Tropics

The flight was from Gatwick airport, London, to Recife. The view from the plane in the early hours of the morning approaching the airport was beyond human comprehension. The sun rose like a huge fireball. Truly Psalm 50:1 was seen to be true:

> *The mighty God, even the Lord, hath spoken, and called the earth from the rising of the sun unto the going down thereof.*

We left Scotland on 11 January 1973, a typical Scottish winter's day, and at six o'clock in the morning we were on Brazilian tropical soil. What a contrast!

Willie hailed a taxi to take us to an address that we had been given. The taxi driver looked at us and said "I don't know if they will be alive at this early hour," I think he meant awake! The address given to us was actually that of a Christian bookshop known as the Christian Literature Crusade. As soon as we arrived we could see activity inside, despite the early hour. All the bookshelves were being put to one side and replaced by seats. They were about to have a meeting!

We were thrilled to the core because of the compassion and vision for perishing souls which these people possessed. No apathy or half-hearted service to God here! By 7am every seat was taken, and outside, the spaces around the windows were occupied; people stood to listen to the gospel being preached. What an inspiration this was to us at the outset of our visit to Brazil!

We hoped to meet the man who ran the bookshop, but he was away on business that day. The preacher was a local Pastor; he preached with great zeal and earnestness. At the end of the service we were able to speak to him. We wondered if this was Bible day or some similar special occasion, but not so! The Pastor told us "I am here Mondays, Wednesdays and Fridays to preach to the people before they start work for the day." Willie told him that in Scotland it would be difficult for us to have a meeting at 7am; unexpressed was the sad thought that it can be difficult to get people out at 7 pm! In reply, the Pastor asked, "Has the salt lost its savour in Scotland?" We were overcome with a sense of guilt—what a challenge to our own hearts and country.

In the congregation was a young lady whose parents were missionaries. She spoke English and Portuguese and made enquiries about our visit. She invited us to her home for lunch, a shower and a rest. Her hospitality was generous, and we welcomed it. Our plane to Belem was not due to leave until the evening; it would have been an exhausting day had we not met this lovely girl and been able to refresh ourselves. God's providence was truly with us.

Renewed Fellowship

We left Recife at 10pm that night and arrived at Belem at 1:30am the next morning. We were warmly greeted by fellow Scottish missionaries. We retired for sleep and were swiftly reminded of our years previously spent in this dear country; it felt strange to be under a mosquito net again, and to have to think twice before drinking the water.

We were told of a new danger; John and Flo Lawson warned us about the rise in crime. Later that morning, as we went down into the town, we were very guarded in all our business.

On the Saturday evening our missionary friends had arranged a surprise dinner for us at a hotel overlooking the river. What a lovely occasion it was of renewed love and fellowship. On the Sunday we were both asked to speak to the children in one of the nearby congregations. What a thrill it was to be back in Brazil and to see so much progress in the work of the gospel.

The text preached by Willie at the conference was taken from John 20:21:

> Then said Jesus to them again, Peace be unto you: as my Father hath sent me, even so send I you.

The disciples' experience of Jesus in verses 20 to 23 is worth a comment. The showing of His hands and side speaks of pardoning and love; this is why they were glad. Yet Jesus goes on! He has made them glad, now he gives them His peace; this was more than a mere greeting – it was a deliberate dispelling of their fear and a sealing of their relationship with Him.

Jesus also commissioned them afresh saying, "As my Father hath sent me, even so send I you," calling them to His purpose, confirming their apostleship, equipping them by the Spirit and preparing them for coming days.

How completely adequate and sufficient is the Risen Lord for the whole of Life!

The Amazon Valley Academy

The conference was to be held at the Amazon Valley Academy (AVA) which is situated in Belem and is a large compound where children of missionaries of many nationalities are taught. It has a high standard of education;

many of the children taught there have gained excellent qualifications and have gained entrance into Universities in their home countries. It is important to remember the teachers and pupils in our prayers; we must pray for the quality of the schooling, and pray that the children will embrace spiritual values. The children of some Brazilian businessmen attend the AVA, and this can only be an influence for good.

During conference week there were a lot of business transactions carried on during the day. New nominations, reshuffling of placements for all the work involved at base, language school, finance, secretaries, teachers, allocation to spheres of service and so on. In the evenings, Willie was responsible for Bible readings. On the first Sunday I had the happy duty of speaking to the Sunday School.

One very important nomination was that of Douglas McAllister, who was elected as field leader. He and his wife, Mary, had been most zealous and conscientious in all areas of their field experience and service. On the last day of the AVA conference Douglas asked Willie to take the communion service, and also to conduct his induction service. He was also called upon to welcome new council members.

At this particular period John and Flo Lawson were engaged in work amongst the Japanese.

The last night of the conference was more like a social evening with the Presentation of Prizes to the pupils and also a presentation to Willie and me. It was a memorable evening with a packed auditorium. We sensed a love and fellowship radiating from that lovely audience of missionaries and their families. Fellowship with God's people is rich and sweet.

A three month tour had been planned for us to visit many of the stations on the river.

Abaetetuba

We went first of all to Abaetetuba for the Women's Conference. This was a real joy, to see so many women who had sacrificed financially to be able to attend and to study God's Word for a whole week. Mr and Mrs Labotz from America accompanied us to share in the ministry at the conference. This was a challenging scene; forty women gathered for a whole week to study the Word of God. They had sacrificed in many ways just to be there; such was their longing and hunger for the Word of God. Mrs Anita Janz was present as a member of the Council and advisor of the Federation. Missionaries present were: Mrs Mary McAllister, Olive Sessom and Joia Hansberger. All of these ladies contributing in their talks to the women. Mary McAllister addressed the Congress; she spoke Portuguese fluently. My part was to speak at the prayer meetings. Willie spoke in the evening on Romans 12:1:

> *I beseech you therefore, brethren, by the mercies of God, that ye present your bodies a living sacrifice, holy, acceptable unto God, which is your reasonable service.*

The Sunday evening meeting was held in the church which was packed. Willie preached on "Can your God deliver you?" It was wonderful to witness three souls making profession of faith at that time.

The following is a quotation from a prayer letter from Joe and Irene Rowley

> "The Abaetetuba course was excellent with all three of us there most of the time. There were around sixty students full time and six graduated on 25th February. Five Guajajara Indians came and did very well. Around twenty-four river regions and churches were represented. Over three hundred ladies were at the Women's Congress and it was encouraging to see ladies from each period of our missionary life, a span of 28 years, most heart warming."

On reading this paragraph from the Rowleys' prayer letter I was greatly encouraged to see how richly God has blessed over so many years.

On returning from Abaetetuba to Belem, John and Flo Lawson kindly did our washing and had it all dried and ironed in no time; we had only hours to go before setting off again.

Cameta and Pindobal

This time we were bound for Cameta which is situated on the River Tocantins. We set off from Belem by launch; Alan Geddes had already gone to prepare the way for our visit. Alan's wife, Rae, with their son Philip, accompanied us. This was my first visit to primitive river dwellings since 1942. The launch was overloaded as usual, a grim reminder of the many privations in such conditions.

On arrival, we met up with Alan and he soon had us sitting comfortably over a cuppa on the veranda of their home.

Sunday morning and evening services were well attended with a congregation of around forty people, and many of the believers gave their testimony. The evening service was broadcast over the loadspeaker system and a young man made a profession of faith. Their new church was under construction and we prayed that every need would be met for its completion.

Alan was an experienced river man; he was fully conversant with launch work and could service the launch himself. He and Willie had been asked to visit a recently converted couple in the Joanna-Peres congregation upstream. I had fully intended to accompany them on the journey but Rae had a high fever and I remained behind to nurse her.

Alan had worked hard to repair a leak in their big launch, but he was unable to complete the repair in time. Alan and Willie set off in a smaller launch and had a pleasant journey upstream. On arrival, they experienced great joy in seeing how God had transformed lives there. The return journey was not so pleasant, indeed it proved strenuous; they had a nasty experience in a rain storm, but thankfully arrived back safely. We then spent a few days in Cameta, preparing for another trip down river to Pindobal.

The big launch was eventually repaired, but as Rae was still unwell and receiving medication, the two men set off for the little congregation. These people were crying out for more teaching from God's Word. They do need our prayers that they will be built up in the faith.

While the men were away, the prayer meeting and Bible study were conducted by one of the deacons. Willie and Alan later returned with splendid reports of the work in Pindobal; two people had been baptised.

Thankfully, Rae's health was improving rapidly.

Belem, Sao Luiz and Barra Do Corda

On returning to Belem from Cameta by launch we had only hours before setting off again. This time we were off to Sao Luiz in the state of Maranhao; we were to travel by plane and then by bus to Barra Do Corda where our seminary was situated.

Jim Vance, one of our missionaries from the seminary met us off the bus. On entering the seminary all the staff gave us a cordial welcome. It was refreshing to discuss with the missionaries all that God had done in the lives of many students who were hoping to be pastors in the near future.

**Students receiving their diplomas at
Barra do Corda**

Guajajara

This was to be a short visit because we were told that our missionaries from the Guajajara Indians were about to arrive to accompany us on the last lap of the journey. Before setting off, we had afternoon tea. We journeyed through the jungle by jeep for about four hours; this was followed by a launch trip.

It was very late when we arrived at Karl and Jeanie Berger's home in the Indian village. Jeanie was most welcoming, providing excellent facilities with which to refresh ourselves. The aroma coming from the kitchen aroused our salivary glands. The meal was excellent. Jeanie and Karl had certainly made a haven of rest in the jungle.

Next day we visited Irene Menzel and Helen Sinclair and saw them at work. Irene carried out medical duties, Helen taught and performed some dentistry. What can we say about these two ladies, undoubtedly doing a heroic work amongst the people?

They visited outlying villages, entailing hazardous journeys through the jungle; they travelled by jeep specially equipped with tools and axes to deal with emergencies – and they had to use them too! On one journey five trees had fallen across their track; Helen and Irene had no choice but to physically hack a way through in order to reach their destination. It is at such times that we sigh and say, "Oh Lord, where are the men to accept such a difficult challenge in such fields of service?"

Nevertheless, we were not discouraged; we saw Guajajara Indians, once steeped in sin and superstition, idolatry and the fear of evil spirits, transformed by hearing the Gospel and receiving Jesus Christ into their lives. Some of these Christians met at 5am for prayer each day because they were concerned about their neighbours! Truly only Jesus Christ can change people from evil practices into renewed beings glorifying His Name.

The Sunday morning was alive with activity. Indians came out of their houses and the call went out over all the village to come to worship – they heeded the call and came. The school house was packed. Oh that we would see in our land such a response to worship on the Lord's Day. At the evening worship Willie preached on "Ye are the salt of the earth," Matthew 5:13, and again there was a good attendance.

How big is your God? Our hearts are saddened here at home to see congregations at evening worship on Sundays halved in number and in some churches there is no evening worship at all. Where is our hunger and thirst after righteousness? Those Guajajara Indians were truly zealous to worship God on His day!

After the service we went to visit a very sick woman in the village. Irene and Helen were also there and they asked me to help with the treatment of this lady. I was delighted to be able to be of service in this manner once again.

Manaos and Tefe

We returned to Belem for a brief respite before travelling by plane to Manaos where Bryn Jones and Jack Mawdsley welcomed us. We spent a few days here with our missionary friends.

Then we were off to Tefe where Bryn and Betty Jones worked; Bryn was with us returning from Belem. This journey was truly out of the ordinary! An American missionary offered us three seats on his float plane. The journey was straightforward – until nature's call caused us to ask the pilot about conveniences!

His response was kind and quick: we suddenly found ourselves landing at the river's edge! At first we thought this a great service but within minutes we were surrounded by a great number of curious people wanting to see the plane and its occupants. All hopes of privacy disappeared. Just another of my embarrassing moments! There have been many such moments while travelling by air, launch and train.

Arriving at Tefe many people gathered to welcome us; they were eagerly looking forward to seeing Bryn again. They helped carry the luggage to Bryn's home where Betty was waiting for us. The congregation was in good heart and services were well attended by men, women and children. Some families had to travel a considerable distance to attend; distance did not hinder their enthusiasm for the gospel.

They sang with all their heart at worship and there was a real hunger for the Word of God. It was a thrilling scene to see many packed canoes arriving for the services. Willie spoke at several services in the church and I spoke at a ladies' meeting.

We received loving hospitality from Bryn and Betty, and renewed our fellowship with them; they had stayed with us on a Deputation tour of Scotland years before. After one of the services they served a meal, inviting some of the congregation – Willie and I especially enjoyed the occasion because it happened to be our wedding anniversary.

Alvaraes

After some days we were off again journeying to Alvaraes, where Robert and Jesse Galbraith were stationed. It was good to see their family so involved in the work; Robert and Jesse being as enthusiastic as ever. At times of worship Robert would be out in the village ringing a bell to call the villagers to church. Robert, Jesse and their family identified themselves with the Brazilians very much, in fact, when on furlough here in Scotland they would get itchy feet to get back home! They have been used of God to plant many churches during their long years of service in Brazil, but as the gospel spread they encountered opposition.

At one time they were tormented by the local priest. Six years later this same priest turned up at the services in Manaos; he came with an ear to hear God's Word! He was awakened to his need for salvation, continued to attend the services and was converted. He then left the priesthood.

Later, he married and had children. Sadly, when still a young man, he became ill – and he was soon to die. Before his death, he expressed his heart's yearning that his wife and family enter into a personal relationship with Jesus Christ. Robert Galbraith conducted the funeral and told us how he wept at the passing of his one-time enemy who had become his friend. There had been a bond of real Christian fellowship between them.

Robert and Jesse have worked faithfully for the sake of the gospel, not counting the cost as we see it, portraying Acts 20:24:

> ... *none of these things move me, neither count I my life dear unto myself...*

They have endured persecutions, separation from their children by thousands of miles because of schooling at the AVA in Belem, and also the loss of one of their children who died in infancy after a sudden onset of illness aboard a launch.

Life is sweet to all of us, and we rightly seek to preserve our health and wellbeing. However, to the missionary, the eye of faith very much governs the way of life, giving holy courage and resolution in the work of taking the gospel to perishing sinners, notwithstanding the difficulties, discouragements and oppositions.

During Robert's time of seeking entrance into new areas he had the dual task of evangelisation and physically building new churches. They had experienced discouragement, but they also had times of uplifting. One outstanding encouragement was seeing one of the Brazilian pastors, Brizido, together with his wife and family, fully in charge of one of those new churches in a very needy area.

We continued the tour of stations on the River Amazon. The launch we journeyed on was named *Maranatha* which means *Our Lord is Coming Soon*. This boat was the one paid for by a businessman in Scotland in the early days of the Mission; it was used for river evangelism, and was an answer to prayer. The missionaries were all skilled in piloting the launch on the River.

The launch serves many functions, the primary one in my mind is that it brings glad tidings to those living in isolated river dwellings! It also acted as an ambulance route in emergencies to take sick people to the nearest hospital. Many dangers lurked in the river, chiefly flotsam which was common due to erosion of the river bank.

On this occasion I experienced a most unpleasant river-related danger. We saw a fisherman in the distance and as we approached we noticed that he had a good catch of fish. This was wonderful provision for us as we had a number of hungry people on board. A deal was done by Robert and we ate a hearty meal of fresh fish. The meal was welcome, but for me the outcome was quite distressing: a fish bone lodged in my throat – it would remain there until removed by a doctor on the following day. In the meantime, I was unable to sleep.

Anori

On the next day we arrived at Anori where Jack and Joan Mawdsley, UFM missionaries, were stationed. Willie arranged for a doctor to examine my throat, and soon I experienced great relief as the offending bone was removed; the doctor prescribed an antibiotic to be given intramuscularly, and Joan administered this course of treatment efficiently.

The Mawdsley's home was undergoing renovations, so we had to sleep on the *Maranatha* whilst the Mawdsleys stayed in the church building. Their baggage had been impounded for some time at Manaos and was only released the day before we departed from Anori. Despite these difficulties, Joan made us welcome and cooked for us all. The meetings at Anori were well attended and Joan's nursing skills were in great demand for the many ailments prevalent in the village.

A few days later we made another trip on the river to a leper colony. Joan visited the colony regularly to give out the appropriate medicine and sought to alleviate the sufferings of these poor people from this disfiguring and crippling disease. Here too was another opportunity to make known the Good News to needy souls.

10. Journey up the Amazon

Kayapos Protest, and Kayapos Wisdom!

Andrew Ballantyne, Deputation Secretary for UFM in Scotland and his wife Anne were serving in Brazil; In 1990 they brought back news of protests by the Kayapos to the General Electric Company in Brazil. The Company were making threats to take Kayapo land. Of course, they highlighted the advantages of their plans; the Kayapos replied by telling them that they could not eat units of electricity! They need the land to cultivate and maintain their livelihood.

In 1973, we had the privilege of visiting the Kayapo Indians. The mode of travel was so much quicker and easier compared to the memorable visit when Willie and Horace Banner travelled by launch and canoe for thirty days. Now we were to be taken by Missionary Aviation Fellowship plane right into the Indian village.

Everything, people and luggage, had to be weighed and checked before the MAF plane took off. The journey began at Anapolis; John Camfield took us to the airport. There was a severe storm at this time so, after three attempts were made to reach the Kayapos, we finally had to turn back to the MAF base.

A fourth attempt was made; we ended up having to make an emergency landing!

The waiting time was difficult, but the pilot was a perfect example of patience and faith. We took accommodation at a hotel and waited for the storm to abate. Waiting time is never easy, but we were reminded of God's rule over the very inclemency of the weather.

I've Seen You Before!

The weather cleared and we were able to fly; we soon arrived safely in the heart of Kayapo territory. The journey that had taken Willie and Horace thirty days in 1936, had taken just three and a half hours!

Kayapo Warrior

When we landed, news spread quickly to all the surrounding area. When we entered the village, now a thriving settlement, we were confronted by many solemn-faced tribesmen.

We asked the chief the reason for all the gloom, his reply was that the Indians had been told in advance that the white visitors had been friends of the missionaries who died at their hands not far from the village.

The solemn expressions were a sign of their humility and shame, and during the next few days, whenever we came face to face with one of these old warriors they would cast down their eyes and sidle past looking awfully sorry for themselves. The fierce reputation of these same men had been enough to put the fear of death into the search party many years before.

We were confronted by a man called Bebo. We stood riveted to the spot as we realised he had something of extreme importance to say to Willie, "I've seen you before," he

Armed Kayapo Warrior

said, and we knew that it could only have been when Willie was on the search with Horace Banner for the missing Three Freds!

We realised he must have had a very good view of Willie from the bush. Of course, he had not seen me because this was my first visit, and Bebo realised that. He went on to question Willie: "How about my old friend Horace?"

Willie told him Horace was very ill and would not be returning to Brazil. At this news Bebo became very emotional and began weeping for his old friend.

He went on, when he was able, to say that Horace had hunted in these forests with him, had fished with him in these rivers and above all he had brought him the good news of the Gospel.

Bebo had been a killer and therefore a warrior of his tribe. We were standing on holy ground; Bebo had been involved in the martyrdom of the Three Freds, yet here he was giving testimony to the saving power of Jesus Christ to transform a savage killer into a redeemed soul. Bebo thanked God for the one who came so many years ago and faithfully proclaimed the Gospel.

Joe Wright, brother of Fred Wright, had once been with his wife Mamie to visit the site of the martyrdom. Speaking through an interpreter, Joe addressed the Kayapo and read from Fred's own Bible. The Kayapo, many of whom had been present at the killing, were impressed that Joe came to them in love, not with hatred and thoughts of revenge; they could not hide their expressions of guilt when they were shown photographs of the Three Freds.

Pombo, a second-in-command and a Christian, spoke in answer. He said that the Kayapo at the time of the killing had been many in number, but were now few in number. He told the Kayapo that Joe and Mamie had come in love, to teach them to love the Lord and to pray. He went on to reprimand some who had been making excuses for not attending church.

On another occasion, Joe, Horace and some Indians trekked to Smoke Falls to visit the very spot where the Freds' boat had been found, and there they held a memorial service.

Go and Sin No More

Next day we visited the home of a man named Chavier who also was a Kayapo Indian. During our conversation he told us that his wife had been unfaithful to him. He was naturally very disturbed and did not know what to do about the matter; he needed some time to contemplate the future. He went off into the jungle for the nut gathering, taking his little radio with him. He hung the radio on a tree, switched it on and heard a sermon from John 8:11:

Neither do I condemn thee: go and sin no more.

These words pierced Chavier's heart and he reached a decision. He returned from the nut gathering to his wife, resolved to show the spirit of forgiveness. Chavier, being a *Jesus Hearer,* listened to His Word and acted upon it. Do we in our worship come with ears to hear? What precious lessons we learn from these humble believers!

Earl and Ivy Trapp, who to this day are engaged in translation work, having spent almost their entire life amongst the Kayapos, are still zealously engaged in the Kayapo outreach. A whole new area has opened for New Testament tapes and also for leaflets with pictures or designs. This was in answer to a request made by the older Indians in far away villages. Other tribes are wanting the same materials and news. They come from areas previously closed to the Gospel, for example, National Park – Upper Xingu. A wonderful testimony to God's Spirit who nurtured seed scattered many years ago and brought it to mature life.

The Enemy of Souls Labours On

Since 1988 the Leadership Training course has been held annually in Sao Felix do Xingu. On two occasions it was held biannually as funds allowed. The latest report of the work in Indian Territory states that some of our missionaries have come under heavy pressure designed to remove them from the tribal areas. The enemy of souls is forever at work to destroy the labours of our missionaries. 1 Peter 5:8 gives us good counsel:

> *Be sober, be vigilant; because your adversary the devil, as a roaring lion, walketh about, seeking whom he may devour:*

Many times missionaries have been blamed for spoiling the culture of the Indian, but some things must be remedied: for example, to extract a tooth the Indian would use the point of a knife to gouge the tooth out – I wonder how we would like that kind of dental treatment!

A Foolish Waste of Time?

A neighbour exclaimed when he heard that Willie was leaving for Brazil: "You are foolish to spend your youth amongst savages. Don't you think we have plenty in our own country who need to hear the Gospel?"

The church in Antioch began with an unexpected group of people. The men of Cyprus and Cyrene were men of vision, boldness, love and obedience; they went beyond the man-made boundaries of Gospel preaching in response to the Lord's commission to all disciples that they were to be his witnesses to all men.

Reader, do you have that breadth of vision, or that depth of obedience? Or are you limited in your view of the extent and power of the Gospel? Have you ever said "It is no use speaking to them, they will never believe?" I wonder what steps we are taking personally and as a church, to reach the unreached?

Nearby, or abroad, the Gospel is not just for *our type of people*; what about other types? Who will tell them of Christ?

A waste of time? What did the three mighty men do for King David? We read in 2 Samuel 23:15, that David longed for a drink from the well of Bethlehem, at that time in Philistine hands. Three men, showing great loyalty for their king, broke into Bethlehem and drew water from the well. They returned to David with it; he was so moved by their gesture that he poured it out as an offering to God. He could not bring himself to drink this invaluable gift.

It is the world that sees a foolish waste of time; Christians see love for their Saviour poured out and being given expression.

11. Rio de Janeiro

Marvellous City

Our last visit before flying home was to Rio de Janeiro where we were able to spend four days. Maurice and Winnie Sloan, with whom we stayed in Janauba, gave us a letter of introduction to the head of a Bible School in Rio. The Principal was a Latvian and though now a widow was bravely running this Bible School. What a warm welcome we received, and the customary cup of coffee was soon served. She calmly sat down with us even though she was exceptionally busy with a full complement of students.

During our conversation our hostess explained that we might find the school living quarters a bit noisy so she had booked us into the Guanabara Hotel for a few days. We were delighted; this was beyond our wildest dreams. She asked one of the students to drive us around some of the important sights on condition that we agree to address the students before leaving for home. Our flight to Gatwick, via Sao Paulo, was the very night of the student meeting she referred to and we were not due to leave Rio until around 11.00pm, so there was just enough time.

Although we had been in Brazil for a number of years, our mission work was in the NorthEast; never during those years did we have the opportunity of such a visit to the South. Here was a golden opportunity to see the sights of Rio de Janeiro!

The Brazilians call this city *Cidade Maravilhosa*, which means marvellous city. The beaches are beautiful with long stretches of sand lined by palm trees. The beach that most easily comes to my mind is the Copacobana beach; it is captivating! One longs to remain for just a moment more to gaze again at the scene; some people playing games and others, relaxing on chairs, simply lapping up the sun. Unfortunately, man spoils this beauty: crowded beaches facilitate theft; one must always be on guard.

The Sugar Loaf Mountain is another great attraction for tourists and provides a breathtaking view of the city.

Corcovado

Television has allowed the world to become familiar with the spectacular view of the Corcovado – a statue of Christ. Designed by a Frenchman, inaugurated in 1931, it rises to a height of 120 feet. Its total weight is 700 tons – the head weighing 30 tons, each arm 30 tons and each hand 8 tons. It is illuminated at night to ensure that it is visible twenty-four hours a day.

The Roman Catholic churches have many huge and imposing buildings here too and the insides contain many very ornate and idolatrous images. These contrast sharply with our evangelical churches which are very plain by comparison.

Outside the city are small shanty towns known as *favelas*; I will never forget the sight of them nestling into the mountain sides of Brazil. Truly Brazil is a land of contrasts. The wealthy in mansions and the poor in shacks. As I looked out of the car window and saw these poor people living in such squalor, I felt that in both of these circumstances, whether wealthy or poverty stricken, it is evident that the need to hear the Gospel is imperative. Romans 10:14:

> How then shall they call on him in whom they have not believed? and how shall they believe in him of whom they have not heard? and how shall they hear without a preacher?

Our time in Brazil was almost over and so we returned to the Bible School on the final evening as arranged. When we entered the Lecture Hall it was packed to capacity. We were overjoyed in our souls to see such zeal in God's work. The sense of God's presence was awesome.

Willie spoke about the work still going on among the Kayapo Indians and how many lives had been transformed by the Gospel. As the meeting closed, we all joined hands from the audience to the platform, singing truly from the heart "God be with you 'till we meet again." Words so appropriate as we were about to journey home.

> Sovereign Ruler of the skies
> Ever gracious, ever wise
> All my times are in Thy hand
> All events at Thy command.
> He that made me at the first
> He shall guide me through the worst
> All my times shall ever be
> Ordered by His wise decree

(Author unknown)

These words brought much comfort and assurance throughout our travels. This last meeting in Rio de Janeiro gripped us just as much as our first meeting in Recife when we witnessed people packing into the bookshop to hear the Word of God.

Sao Paulo Reunion

We re-routed our homeward journey in order to make an overnight stop in Sao Paulo. Our main reason for this was to meet a young Brazilian lad named Oswaldo whom we first met in Canniesburn Hospital, Glasgow.

While serving in the Brazilian army he had sustained a serious hand injury. The army had made many enquiries at hospitals in various countries because they realised that only specialist skill could restore the injured hand. Canniesburn Hospital specialises in plastic surgery, and is renowned throughout the world, so Oswaldo was sent off to Scotland.

On admission to hospital the staff were unable to communicate with him; he could speak no English, they could speak no Portuguese. He could not converse with surgeons, nurses, dieticians, or anyone who needed information in order to look after his welfare. Someone knew of Willie, knew that he had been in Brazil and could speak Portuguese fluently, so a message was sent asking him to help. When Willie came to Oswaldo's bedside and spoke to him in Portuguese the response was effervescent; Oswaldo exclaimed "You have the key to all doors!"

Willie did indeed have the key – but in more ways than Oswaldo knew. Willie could unlock the barrier between Oswaldo and the Canniesburn staff, and also, by the Spirit's power, unlock the barrier to Heaven.

The surgical treatment required a fairly long stay in hospital. The ensuing daily visits opened doors for witness about the Great Physician who can heal the sin-sick soul. Oswaldo read a Portuguese New Testament twice during his stay in hospital. The day he was discharged we arranged for him to come to our home for a meal. After the meal he made known his desire to follow Christ.

Now you can understand why we so wanted to visit Sao Paulo.

Our reunion was in the usual demonstrative Brazilian style, *abraco apertadissimo*, which means a tight hug, and that visit was so memorable. We were just sorry that it had to be so short.

What a reminder we have here of God working out His purposes in bringing this lad from the army in Brazil to a bed in Canniesburn Hospital where he could have a one-to-one talk about the saving Power of our God.

Never doubt that God rules and reigns in His Heaven despite what some may say; Psalm 93:1:

> The Lord reigneth, he is clothed with majesty; the Lord is clothed with strength, wherewith he hath girded himself: the world also is stablished, that it cannot be moved.

How good it was to be back in Scotland again, safe with family, friends and especially the church, where we could again be built up by the ministry of the Word. Here was a fresh opportunity to relate to many churches all that God had been doing and was doing throughout Brazil.

12. Retired or Re-tyred?

UFM Farewell to Willie

In 1976, after almost 46 years of service, a UFM Fare-well evening was organised for Willie by Mrs Marion Small, Secretary in the Glasgow UFM office at that time. Many of our former colleagues on the field were there including Rev and Mrs Leonard Harris, Joe and Maimie Wright, Lily Heath, Bob and Alma McAllister, as well as our own family members. There was a good representation from all the various Mission Halls and churches throughout Scotland where Willie had formerly preached.

The Rev. Douglas MacMillan, who was our minister at St Vincent Street, spoke on behalf of the St Vincent Street congregation and we had a grand time. Willie was presented with a music centre and I received a nest of tables and a tea service. The people of the Shetland Isles gifted a travel rug, Caithness folk gifted Caithness glass vases, and the saints in Inverness a beautiful picture of Glencoe. Our daughter Heather presented Mrs Small with a bouquet of flowers. Such thoughtfulness and kindness shown was never to be forgotten.

We had so many people staying overnight that our good Christian neighbours, Mr and Mrs Chalmers, gave help by providing additional accommodation, and warm hospitality, to those who required it for the night.

Willie always joked about the word *retired* saying *re-tyred*, as his wish was still to be active in God's work.

Lennoxtown

In 1978 St Vincent Street Free Church of Scotland was asked if they would take over an Independent Church in the village of Lennoxtown as an outreach. Lennoxtown's population is in the region of 3000 souls. This church had

been a faithful witness for 24 years under the ministry of
Mr and Mrs Gordon Buckley. After the death of Mrs
Buckley, Mr Buckley was led to give St Vincent Street a
very generous offer of the church building, which is situated in the Main Street, nestling under the Campsie Hills.

When the Kirk Session gathered to consider this offer,
Rev Douglas MacMillan proposed that Willie take up the
challenge. Willie prayerfully considered this; he accepted
and thereby took on yet another demanding role in life.

An elder and a deacon were assigned to Lennoxtown by
rota each Sunday from St Vincent Street. Two deacons
with their wives and families volunteered to come to Lennoxtown for a longer period. They were Mr Allister Mac-
Lean and his wife Nancy with their two sons Jonathan
and Kenneth, and Mr George Gilgis and his wife Heather,
our daughter, with their two children, Gillian and Judith.
George was faithful as precentor and Heather taught in
the Sunday School.

The hardness of men's hearts reminded us of our early
days in Parnaiba, Brazil. However, the aforementioned
folk helped us enormously; there was a great deal of fer-
vent prayer. Many personal contacts were made by door-
to-door visitation. Others also laboured with us. Francis
and Susan Brown had been very faithful workers when
the Buckley's laboured and they continued their untiring
support, labouring in the Gospel. Sheila MacLeod who
was from Balfron was a great asset to our congregation in
many ways and Mr Stangoe, an elderly gentleman also
contributed in many lovely ways.

An Irish family who had a farm in Killearn joined in
our worship regularly and encouraged us, as did Eric
Stewart and his fiancee. Others who helped in the work
were Mr and Mrs Hatch, and Donald and Murdina MacLeod and family from the Bishopbriggs Free Church congregation.

Our first communicant member was Jim Clark, followed by Ann MacDonald from Point, on the Isle of Lewis,

and Ann Eadie who came regularly to church with Ann MacDonald.

After attending a never-to-be-forgotten Communion service, Derek, Ann Eadie's husband, was observed to leave the service rather hurriedly. That same evening as we came out to the service he met me at the car and said, "I would like to come to the prayer meeting on Wednesday." I exclaimed, "Oh, that would be great!" Truly the Spirit of God had been doing His silent work. Derek continued, "I was converted this afternoon!"

Another Work of the Spirit was Mrs MacDonald, the cleaner at the church, who also made known her desire to follow Christ.

In 1980, Willie was showing signs of being unwell. The doctor having examined him prescribed tablets for one month. At the end of this period there was no improvement so further investigations were carried out which indicated that surgery was necessary. Happy to say that he made a speedy and successful recovery.

There was a great deal of darkness in Lennoxtown with respect to the Gospel. There was a time when church property was highly respected; however, vandalism to our little church was now all too common. Sadly, this is an indication of a godless society. So, the work was mixed with both discouragements and encouragements. Nevertheless, our trust was in the Living God and so we were confident that His Word would not return to Him void. As Psalm 126:6 says:

> *He that goeth forth and weepeth, bearing precious seed, shall doubtless come again with rejoicing, bringing his sheaves with him.*

Members came and members went but this served to reaffirm our dependency upon God rather than on any individual. Our duty is to be faithful in the proclamation of the Gospel. God, who sees the end from the beginning will glorify His Name in it all.

The time came for a younger minister to labour in Lennoxtown and Rev Ian Beaton was inducted to the charge around 1983. The induction service was taken by Rev Peter Jackson and Rev William MacLeod; Ian has a very capable wife, Margaret, who is a great support in the work.

The night of Ian's induction was a night to remember. The church was packed with many who had shown interest in the work. It was a dual occasion; the members of our little church wanted to display in a visible manner their esteem for us as we departed. Inductions in the Free Church are always carried out with great dignity and spirituality.

The ladies of both St Vincent Street and Lennoxtown congregations had also made great preparation for tea and fellowship.

We returned to St Vincent Street to worship but George and Heather and the Eadie family continued a bit longer and Allister and Nancy MacLean are still worshipping and helping in the Lennoxtown congregation, as are Mr Eric Stewart, his wife and family.

Deep Spiritual Fellowship

Willie continued serving the Lord at St Vincent Street and he was also involved in the Foreign Missions Board of the Free Church, travelling through to Edinburgh to attend Committee meetings. This gave him great pleasure and, at the end of such a day, on hearing the key in the door, I would run to meet him and he would say, "It's your wee man back home."

Although we had returned to St Vincent Street Church, Willie was away most weekends engaged in pulpit supply in various parts of the country; I often accompanied him.

We had such lovely times of deep spiritual fellowship and found that many people enjoyed speaking of the things of the Kingdom. Malachi 3:16:

Then they that feared the Lord spake often one to another: and the Lord hearkened, and heard it, and a book of remembrance was written before him for them that feared the Lord, and that thought upon his name.

Willie & Cathie, Inverness

He was also involved in UFM Council meetings once a month and that involved rising at 5.30am to get the shuttle plane from Glasgow to Heathrow airport in London arriving there for 9am. This was always a long tiring day, between travelling and so much talking at these meetings. However, it was always carried out with much dedication. I think very often that we forget the many hours that God's servants spend in all the business transactions of the church. They are all most important and we should pray for these meetings that wisdom may be given in all deliberations.

In Mrs Mackenzie's Garden, Inverness

Hanover Housing Accommodation – 1985

In the spring of 1985 I was quite unwell with a viral infection, resulting in a fair loss of weight and general debility. Thoughts were prompted about a smaller house and it so happened that the Hanover Housing Association were in their final stages of building sheltered housing flats fairly near to where we lived. We committed the thought of a possible move to God. The thought of a smaller house was uppermost at this time so we applied for one of the 41 flats in the complex. We were successful in our application and moved into our new home in May 1985.

We had only been there a few days when the Warden said that the residents would like to have a church service there. Willie was overjoyed and felt honoured to be asked to minister the Word at a service in the Common room once a month; it was quite well attended. One of our residents who supported Willie in this work, Mr Robin Ewing, is, at the time of writing, in charge of getting different speakers each month from various churches. The Word of God is still being heard each month and we continue to pray that the good seed sown will bear fruit.

Willie met a man in Glasgow from the Scottish Commercial Travellers' Christian Union. He mentioned that he was holding services at Hanover Gardens and felt there was a need for Bibles to be available in each home there. This man came to the complex and spoke to the residents one day about the Christian Union; at the end he presented a specially inscribed Bible to each home.

My Illness – 1988

One Sunday following the morning service I collapsed in the street on leaving St Vincent Street Free Church. Willie had gone in front with one of our granddaughters, Elaine. George and Heather were with me and helped me to the car. I was taken to Stobhill Hospital Casualty Department and admitted to the Coronary Care Unit where I was diagnosed as having angina. I was given further tests and treatment at Glasgow Royal Infirmary and treated with the utmost skill and kindness; I am thankful to say that I am now reasonably well, provided I get adequate rest.

During that time of being hospitalised and confined to bed I liked to read. Bishop J C Ryle brought me much peace and calmness of spirit. He says in his commentary, "Faith never rests so calmly and peacefully as when it lays its head on the pillow of God's omnipotence." To this moment, I have found the quotation a constant comfort in many perplexing situations in life.

Golden Wedding Celebration – 1990

On 1 March 1990 we celebrated our Golden Wedding in a quiet family atmosphere at a local hotel.

**Christie, Donald, Heather & Leslie
Willie & Cathie**

We looked back on our years together and considered how our family had grown – four children and nine grand-children. Leslie had trained in the Glasgow shipyards, and had then joined the Metropolitan Police where he served until he retired in January 1996. Donald became a minis-ter with the Church of Scotland, Christie a carpenter with his own business, and Heather studied at Edinburgh Uni-versity before becoming a teacher.

We were all brought into reflective mood as the family highlighted various incidents throughout their lives and ours.

Willie and I were both living on borrowed time so we had much to praise God for, to enjoy our children and grandchildren, not forgetting our friends at St Vincent Street who also shared in our joy, with all their different expressions of love and kindness.

Dark Days Ahead

Two days later, at 11am on 3 March 1990, my brother James phoned to say how much he had enjoyed the Golden Wedding and went on to say, "I think Ada and I will do the same," their anniversary fell on the following year.

At 2pm that same day we received a telephone call from Ada to say Jim had collapsed and died on returning from the shops; Jim had been a great influence on me in my early Christian life.

On 15 April Willie was preaching at Dunoon Free Church. We had both sensed God's presence in worship and we received warm hospitality from the dear folks of the church. After the service, on leaving the church building, I fell down the stairs sustaining a fractured fe-mur and was taken to Dunoon Hospital for X-ray.

As I looked at my husband, now eighty years old, I could see poor Willie was truly shaken by the sudden change of events; he was exhausted in any case, having preached three times that day between Dunoon and Strachur. We were grateful to the session clerk Mr MacAuley and to the staff at Dunoon Hospital who set in motion all the necessary arrangements for me to be admitted to Glasgow Royal Infirmary. Thankfully, skilled treatment and nursing soon had me on the road to recovery.

On 22 May my eldest brother, Willie, died quite suddenly and my sister-in-law, Ada, was in hospital seriously ill, the prognosis being bleak.

Willie's Last Illness

In July 1990, while preparing to go on holiday, Willie was not at all well. However, despite my earnest request to cancel the holiday he assured me he would be all right. Heather, George and the girls were going with us to a caravan in the Lake District. The whole journey was difficult but we eventually arrived safely.

At midnight Willie awoke in great distress and required a doctor urgently. George contacted the warden and within ten minutes the doctor was in attendance. She administered medication which brought Willie wonderful relief. The doctor returned next morning and advised him to stay indoors all that day, Sunday, but if the weather was favourable on the Monday we could go out for a bit.

The Monday turned out to be such a lovely day that we all went for a picnic at Ambleside. Following our return to the caravan I had an angina attack and again George had to call the doctor. The doctor returned next morning and strongly advised the two of us to go home. We had a safe journey home and contacted our own doctor. Many hospital tests followed over a period of three months but Willie's condition deteriorated quite rapidly.

On 25 September 1990, Willie was called home to be with his Lord whom he loved so dearly and whom he had served so faithfully.

I was deeply grieved after Willie's death, and comforted very much by my family and friends. The Gospel of John 14:27 states:

> *Peace is what I leave with you; I do not give it as the world does. Do not be worried and upset; do not be afraid.*

Now I was most conscious of that inner peace which nothing can destroy.

Another *Path* had yet to be taken, with the Comforter alongside to lead and direct me to new horizons.

To God be All Praise and Glory

In the month of May 1995, I was highly privileged and honoured to celebrate my 80th birthday. My family had secretly arranged a very special family gathering at a hotel not too distant from my home.

A beautiful meal was served, and as the evening unfolded, I was truly overwhelmed by their love displayed with overflowing generosity. Elaine, my youngest granddaughter presented me with a beautiful bouquet of flowers.

The special occasion ended with reflections of God's mercies and faithfulness throughout so many years – to God be all the Praise and Glory.

13. Epilogue

Since coming home from Brazil after the war years, the apathy I have observed in many of our churches and a general lack of commitment to serve God is in such a contrast with that meeting for worship we attended in Recife in 1973, where we saw a people being obedient as the psalmist in Psalm 119:112 says:

> I have inclined mine heart to perform thy statutes alway, even unto the end.

Only hearty service pleases the Lord and the believers of Recife were willing and eager to serve Him.

In Psalm 119:105 we read:

> Thy Word is a lamp unto my feet and a light unto my path.

Do you want to know which *Path of Life* you should take? So many people when asked this question begin by saying "I think..." which confirms they have left God out of their lives. *God's Word* is our only authority for a pattern of behaviour wherever we may be placed in life. The great William Tyndale gave his life in order that we might know the *Path of Life* through translating the Bible into the English language.

Let us look again into the Brazilian jungle, consider prayerfully the latest news, and present before the Lord the prayer requests of His servants.

In the following prayer letter, you will find up-to-date news from Eva Banner. She and Horace have spent 40 years in Brazil amongst the Kayapos. They laboured at a most difficult task. In looking at many reports of those days and comparing with the reports of today, truly the seed sown in tears has brought a wonderful harvest of souls, Psalm 126:6:

> He that goeth forth and weepeth, bearing precious seed, shall doubtless come again with rejoicing, bringing his sheaves with him.

Eva Banner's Prayer Letter:

Prayer News of the Kayapo Indians – July 1994

This year we have marked the 500th anniversary of the birth of William Tyndale, the man who translated the Bible into the English language in defiance of a law which prohibited anyone from doing so. Brazil's Indians face the prospect of similar restrictions today, though many, including the Kayapo, already have New Testaments, due to the work of Wycliffe Bible Translators and other missions. Please pray for the Indians, noting the following four points:

1. "Rede Globo" the most popular TV network in Brazil, recently revealed a document from the World Council of Churches which was said to advocate political subversion amongst the Indians. This made viewers think that Christians had infiltrated the Indian people for political purposes which would actually be harmful to them. In Portuguese, the name "World Council of Churches" is similar to that of the Unevangelized Fields Mission World-Wide and its associate churches in Brazil, so some people have represented the mission as an enemy to the Indians. (Some Indians have heard this and believed it.) Members of the mission have, therefore, had to try to convince the authorities that no evangelical mission would identify itself with the WCC. In fact, UFM has always had good relations with the government's Indian Foundation agency.

The WCC document dated from 1981 and is 13 years out of date, but it was presented as if it was new!

Pray that the damage done to relationships between missions, authorities and the Indians may be repaired and that the mission will be vindicated.

2. A byelaw has been signed by the Minister of Justice which virtually prohibits religious literature in the languages of the tribes and imposes censorship. This law could make continued work by the missions amongst the Indians very difficult. It could also hinder further progress with literacy.

Pray that God will overrule in this matter and that Bible and Christian literature will continue to be available to the Indian people in their own language.

3. Some people in the church at Gorotire decided that the Bible in Portuguese was the only reliable one and urged others in the church to use it, even though many did not fully understand Portuguese. This came through outside pressure from non-Kayapo speaking people. If this was applied (as with the byelaw), Kayapo Christians would cease to be edified and the church would effectively be unable to function.

Pray that wise counsels will prevail among church leaders.

4. During the absence of the missionaries while they were away on furlough, people from a church group in a new mining town some distance away made overtures to the Gorotire Church, promising a new church building and a salary for the pastor, who is currently unpaid, if the church will change its affiliation. The Rede Globo programme had left the members of Gorotire Church thinking that the missionaries were not returning, so this approach caused much confusion and had led to a power struggle within the church.

Pray that the influence of this group, which lacks knowledge of the language and culture of the people, will be checked and that the church will not fall into the trap of responding to the appeal of material benefits which would be secured at the cost of the Church's spiritual integrity.

A more uplifting situation is found in a UFM prayer letter from John and Flo Lawson dated September 1994.

"This is a letter of rejoicing in what the Lord is doing in our midst. In our last letter we wrote that we were concerned about the little congregation that we attend in New City 8 (near Belem). The Lord has answered our prayer and several people have accepted the Lord in recent weeks... Another encouraging note is that each weekend we have the help of two students from the Word of Life Bible Institute. They are members of the Maraba church. Already their cheerful spirits have brought an uplift to the congregation and they are very *positive* in their *input* in all that they do."

The Church in Brazil - 1994

Bryn Jones, UFM Council member, sums up well the condition of the church in Brazil:

"One more, Brazil" was the cry from the television as the nation was winding itself up for the World Cup months in advance. This was in stark contrast to the financial crisis that the country was facing with devaluation of the currency being on a daily basis of 1.5%. The political scandals were part of the daily news with many senior politicians facing major charges of corruption.

To visit again for two months was both an exhilarating and a very depressing experience. To meet friends is always a joy especially after so many years. The Field Conference in Belem was the usual routine of meetings and meetings and more meetings. However, this year one item dominated, namely the future of field headquarters.

Administration and the education of children does not have the same appeal to the Christian public as launch evangelism, or working with the street children, but unless the field is able to manage these areas then other work suffers. The situation of the headquarters, and the school for the children of missionaries in Belem has resulted in a very large percentage of the workers being in the state capital. Headquarters and schools are there for the sake of the Gospel and the reaching of Brazilians with the Gospel.

Unless the Church is being encouraged, enriched and enabled then no superstructure is defensible.

What about the Church in Brazil? No one can truly answer that question for it is as varied in practice and theology as East is from West. In addition, the geographical expanse of the country means that no one person can ever have a meaningful knowledge of the work. Of the area of the work formerly known as the West Amazon it is possible to make an appraisal.

Numerically, the Church has prospered beyond expectation. Villages that had no Gospel witness have thriving churches with many faithful Christians but ... The 'but' is a very serious 'but'. Churches are showing all the signs of division, in-fighting and lack of spiritual leadership. Betty and I were heartbroken to be in town when a major eruption was taking place between the present pastor and a previous retired pastor who was unable to accept changes. (That would never happen in this country would it!)

On our last Sunday in Tefe the pastor resigned, the church divided with terrible bitterness and the cause of the Gospel was set back years in the town. What a tragedy when we remember the sacrifice of the early missionaries and the faithfulness of the Christians as they suffered persecution and insults for their faith. What shame when we consider the enormous dedication of many believers in seeing the Church growing to congregations of hundreds on a Sunday and to have the Prefect (full-time executive Mayor) of town, the first Christian Prefect in the history of the town as a member of the church.

Caridade, formerly known as Jacare, has few problems in comparison and through our rose-tinted glasses it shines out from the high bank of the Amazon river. It is 25 years since we first preached the Gospel in that little village. On the first night eight people trusted the Lord and what a transformation the preaching of the Gospel has brought to that village.

From a group who could not hold their heads up in society because of extreme poverty, caused not only because of the environment but through their wasteful life style, there has emerged a thriving church with excellent local leadership. Resident missionaries or national workers are almost unheard of in Caridade. Jean Allen (nee Bradshaw) and Phyllis MacLean spent six months teaching the adults to read; this was a major turning point in the development of the work.

The leader, Francisco, is one of the eight converted on the first night. He is a great influence in the village and community and is now serving his second term as a councillor on the local administrative council.

The progress of the Gospel can well be illustrated by the number of buildings that have been erected for worship. It all started with a thatched roof shack with no walls: today a brick building with Sunday School rooms is nearing completion.

Similar stories of sorrow and joy could be encountered in other centres like Alvaraes, Anori and Maraa. The Church needs dedicated leaders as pastors and deacons if it is to be faithful to the Word of God and avoid some of the extreme ways that are becoming common in some of the churches. Numerically the church is thriving, but superficiality and worldly methods are areas of great concern. Added to this there is a grave deficiency in evangelism and the process of becoming Christians.

Part of my sabbatical was to read Brazilian authors and their view of the Church. To emphasise my point, one of the authors, a well known evangelist in Brazil, believes that today there are more people who have made a profession of faith who never attend church than there are people in Church on Sunday.

"One more, Brazil!" is history now. They have won one more Cup but what of the Church – is it winning? Numerically yes, but whether it is really the "salt or light" of Brazil is an open question and one that should cause us to support and pray for those who are seeking to bring to that land a Biblical basis to the Church.

Bryn Jones.

Where Others Would Not Go

Today the Kayapo tribe have a high percentage of Christians, and so have many other Brazilian tribes contacted since the 1930s by the Mission. Many wondered why we laboured for Brazilian Indian souls and not for the unconverted nearer home.

Willie's response was that the Bible teaches that apart from Christ there is no salvation. Further, we know that there were people who would never hear of Christ because of the problems of language and the wild nature of culture and environment; stark savages in unexplored territory, they would never hear – unless His teaching was carried to them: Matthew 28:19

Go ye therefore, and teach all nations, baptizing them in the name of the Father, and of the Son, and of the Holy Ghost.